Also by Alysa VanderWeerd:

Mountaintop Mornings

Life.

ALYSA VANDERWEERD

WESTBOW
PRESS®
A DIVISION OF THOMAS NELSON
& ZONDERVAN

WestBow Press books may be ordered through booksellers or by contacting:

WestBow Press
A Division of Thomas Nelson & Zondervan
1663 Liberty Drive
Bloomington, IN 47403
www.westbowpress.com
1 (866) 928-1240

ISBN: 978-1-9736-0696-3 (sc)
ISBN: 978-1-9736-0697-0 (hc)
ISBN: 978-1-9736-0695-6 (e)

Library of Congress Control Number: 2017916824

Print information available on the last page.

WestBow Press rev. date: 11/16/2017

Dedicated to my future man who is taking Forever.
And. A. Day. to come into the picture.
But worth the wait!

To my hot and humble future husband God has set apart,
Here is my heart.

<3

Hope this gets to you

"If you look up into His face and say, 'Yes, Lord, whatever it costs,' at that moment He'll flood your life with His presence and power."

~Alan Redpath

Author's Preface

I wouldn't necessarily call myself a poet. I had writer's block.

I could not for the life of me work on the book that had been on my heart for years. You set aside time, you sit or stand behind your computer, and nothing. No words come. The struggle can be overwhelming. That feeling, "I'm wasting so much time!" There are those times in life when the words you want won't come, so you need to just write something; you never know, that something may be pretty amazing. It could be: journaling, a free flow of thought, writing your prayers to God, or taking a topic and writing down everything you know about that specific subject.

I have a habit of writing my prayers to God. It helps me focus and concentrate. Oftentimes, as I am writing out my prayers, my heart to God in that moment, He will impress my heart with a word or a direction for my writing. Whenever you are seeking to use your gift, my encouragement is that you would begin in prayer. As you simply talk to the Lord and hear His voice, He, by the power of the Holy Spirit opens your eyes to gaps that need to be filled. He highlights scripture. He gives you a vision. He tells you, "Go!"

> Anointed works are bathed in prayer.
> They begin in prayer;
> They are filled with prayer;
> They end in prayer.

Sometimes, I talk too much, and the Lord sweetly reminds me to stop talking and listen. Those moments, I stop and take in His love as I read His words of truth. I believe the Lord longs to have those long uninterrupted conversations with us; a dialogue, not a monologue. He loves hearing our voice just as much as He loves speaking into our situation. Most of my poems came when I was praying or reading a specific piece of scripture.

I have a quirk of always needing the alphabet by me when I am working on poems. I keep it scrawled on a sticky note next to my computer. A thought would come, I would look at the alphabet and then I would just write and these poems are what came at that time.

Totally the Lord. A gift of His grace. For His glory alone!

These poems became almost like my prayer journal, as I talked to God and read His word and wrote. I'm definitely not perfect. I face the crazy in life just like you. Love the fact that God gives us outlets to express what is going on inside of us; He doesn't condemn us and He does not waste our pain. Those outlets of expression may reach more people than you can even imagine—**Ephesians 3:20.**

For God takes the impact of a life,
    and it continues on to generations because of Christ.

When I was struggling with writer's block in October of 2015, I was reading through my second chapter in my purity book that talks about holiness. I was stuck as I was trying to define holiness in simple terms. J.C. Ryle has a 400-page book on holiness. My goal was to explain it in a couple of pages. The struggle is real. Seriously. I was stuck. All I could think about was that holiness encompasses a set apart life. People who are set apart leave legacies for generations to come, solely because Jesus Christ fills their life. I was thinking about legacies and I was reminded of a hashtag I posted a couple of months prior for a photograph I put on Instagram: #toGodbetheglorygreatthingsHehasdone. The first line of one of my favorite hymns by Fanny Crosby, "To God Be the Glory." And the Lord gave me this line for the next hashtag: #andgreatthingsHeisgoingtodothroughChristHisSon. God has done great things in the past, but He is currently doing great things now and will continue to do great things through Jesus Christ. God is ever present in the life of a Christian. Jesus Christ is moving through Christians right now impacting for eternity's time.

People who are set a part hear Christ and in the gift God has given them, their outlet of expression reaches many for the glory of God. The two hashtags kept going through my head, as I was thinking about legacies; and that's how my first poem came, *Until the End*. We do not know the number of our days. But what we do know is that until Jesus Christ comes back or calls us home, He's given us "legacy-leaving work" to accomplish.

What's your legacy-leaving work?

We may never see the impact of our life until heaven. Every life is valuable. Jesus Christ died for our very life; so that we might live today through eternity. And He has given us gifts to use. Your gift may differ than your brothers' or sisters' gift and that is what is so awesome. I love to write. But it can be difficult at times, as any gift is. God is greater than our difficulty; He truly brings beauty from ashes.

From struggle came inner strength—**Ephesians 3:16,**
    As I clung to Christ through trial and pain.

God knows what you can handle. So, my prayer for you today, knowing how difficult and yet how beautiful life is; is that you would use the gifts God has given you to shine, solely for His glory. He is with you always—**Matthew 28:20.**

God Bless you all!
::*Alysa VanderWeerd*, 2017

INTRODUCTION

My book of poems— Life,
All describe aspects of heroic endurance.
What to do in life,
When we are constantly tested under trial and strife.

God blesses the people, (**James 1:12**)
Who patiently endure testing,
Who endure temptation,
Who remain steadfast under trial,
Holding fast to Christ;
Those will be the ones who receive the crown of life.

The reward for enduring,
Clinging to Christ,
Is Life.

Many succumb and cave amidst the battle.
The temptations are strong,
The testing making one feel unstable,
Moving them to bail,
When God wants them to remain able.

But those who patiently endure,
Persevering in prayer;
The reward is Life.
Eternal Life is theirs.
That's the gift,
Given by Christ,
Every crown describes,
A characteristic of the afterlife,
And this crown for enduring trial,
Is the Crown of life.
Eternal life.

There will be a day,
When you cast that crown Christ's way.
Recognizing it was solely Jesus,
Who gave you the strength to endure the day.

Jesus Christ reigns,
He gives strength to all,
Who seek Him above all,
He hears and answers every call.

So, I encourage you today,
When times of trial come your way,
Cling to Christ and His Word,
As Jesus' precious name and presence answers,
Every overwhelming trial,
Becoming your greatest treasure.

Heroic endurance is not quitting or bailing out on what God has called you specifically to do. Life is a gift from God. Every life is a miracle. Life is not always easy. But whether we are on the mountaintop or in the valley God wants us all passionately seeking Him—**Jeremiah 29:13,** obeying His voice—**John 14:15.**

The poems in this book are presented in the order of when I wrote them. Some are prayers. Some are not prayers. The word on my heart in that moment. The stream of thought throughout this book simply shares Life.

The Bible brings *life* alive.

As the psalmist declares, "This is my comfort in my affliction, for Your word has given me life"—**Psalm 119:50.** It validates our meaning and existence. A special treasure from our King to guide us in every endeavor. I include a lot of verses next to my poems. The Bible, God's heart to us, is the greatest book to read. My prayer is that as you read through these poems and your eye catches a verse that you would be encouraged to open up the Word of God to read and experience His absolute love for you. You are His personal concern—**1 Peter 5:7**.

When I was praying about how to choose what poems to include the Lord reminded me of Gideon's 300. The Lord tested the men by bringing them to the water—**Judges 7:4**. How did they handle the water? The ones God chose cupped the water with their hands; they took a sip, looked around, took another sip. Like a Berean on guard searching the Scriptures—**Acts 17:11**. When I read the word "water," I am reminded of *living water*— the Holy Spirit—**John 4:10-11**. That which is filled with the Spirit is lasting—**2 Corinthians 3:5-6**. I am also reminded of "washing of water by the word"—**Ephesians 5:26**. The Word of God is cleansing; it is sanctifying. I wanted my poems to reflect these characteristics; Holy Spirit filled while cleansing and sanctifying, full of God's Word. In **Judges 7**, God separated the men by how they handled the water. The men He did not choose went to their knees and stuck their face into the water. They weren't on guard; kind of like people who take everything at face-value without checking the facts. People make mistakes. God alone is perfect. It is fun searching the Scriptures for Truth!

Jesus is returning! Right now, I believe the greatest expression of our love for Him, is living His heart found in the Word. As you read through these poems, I pray your heart gets ignited to live God's heart to the next level!

KNOW GOD

What is the meaning of *life*?
Why am I here?
Why do I face countless crazy trials and issues in *life*?
Where am I supposed to be?
When will I die?
How am I supposed to live this thing called *life*?

In **John 14:6** Jesus says, "I am the way, the truth, and the life. No one comes to the Father except through Me." Jesus Christ is the life. Our meaning comes from knowing Him. It is a relationship with the Savior that reigns; the King of Kings. You are here right now to know Him—**John 17:3**. You face countless crazy trials and issues in life because there is sin in the world. Adam and Eve, seriously, their one choice changed life for everyone—**Genesis 3**. By choosing to eat of the forbidden fruit, sin entered the world. There is not one perfect person walking this earth. Everyone sins. All have fallen short of the glory of God—**Romans 3:23**. But the fact is, God is so holy and just that He cannot look upon sin—**Habakkuk 1:3**. He does not wink at sin. Your sin is a wall separating you from God on High—**Isaiah 59:1-2**. You need a Savior.

God knew this would happen. Even with perfect knowledge of your sin, He still loves you. So, in His love He sent His perfect Son, Jesus Christ, to be born of a virgin and to walk this earth. The Bible says, "For the wages of sin is death, but the gift of God is eternal life in Christ Jesus our Lord"—**Romans 6:23**. You deserve to pay the ransom for your sin. There is no forgiveness of sin without the shedding of blood—**Hebrews 9:22**; sin must be paid for with precious lifeblood to make atonement for your very soul—**Leviticus 17:11**. But God loves you! He sent His Son, Jesus Christ, to die on the cross to shed His own blood to forgive your sin. Love paid it for you! Jesus stepped in and paid your debt with His own precious lifeblood—**1 Peter 1:18-19**. But He didn't stay dead, He rose again three days later—**1 Corinthians 15:3-4**; and is now sitting at God's right hand interceding specifically for you—**Hebrews 1:3**. Jesus lives to intercede for you—**Hebrews 7:25**. It's just what He does. You can't escape His prayers. He knows the weight of your sin is holding you down, keeping you from enjoying an abundant life here on earth and from the hope of heaven—**Hebrews 12:1**. He wants you walking freely—**Galatians 5:13**. He wants you to be with Him in heaven one day—**1 Timothy 2:4**.

Today, is the day of salvation—**2 Corinthians 6:2**.

Your life is valuable to God. Jesus Christ died for your very life. He loves you! But in His love He allows you to choose whether to love Him back. He alone knows the day of your death. He alone knows the day of Christ's return. He is waiting patiently for many to repent, but there is a day when the waiting game ends—**2 Peter 3:9**. Hell is real. You have a choice of choosing eternal life in heaven with Jesus Christ face to face, or eternity in hell.

Choose Life.

1 John 1:9 says, "If we confess our sins, He is faithful and just to forgive us our sins and to cleanse us from all unrighteousness."

Realize you are a sinner—**Romans 3:23**
Recognize that Jesus Christ died on the cross for you—**Romans 5:8**
Repent of your sin—**Acts 3:19**
Receive Christ into your life—**Romans 10:9.**

If you want to accept Jesus Christ into your heart today,
All you have to do is pray:

Jesus, would You forgive me of my sin?
I recognize You as my Lord and Savior whose blood covers my sin.
Thank you for dying on the cross and rising again.
Please help me to follow you every day of my
life amongst these men and women.
Thank You for saving me today,
In Jesus' precious name, Amen.

Life.

1. Until the End

October 2, 2015

To God be the glory,
Great things He has done.
And great things He is going to do
Through Christ His Son.

He moves through His children,
He sets them apart.
He tells them His secrets,
So they know His heart.

He says, "Go into all the world,
And make disciples of men.
Preach the gospel,
Until the end."

The set apart Christian knows Christ is coming back,
And their days are few,
To accomplish the legacy-leaving work
God has called them to.

2. Set Free

November 13, 2015

You know me so well,
And you love me still.
You know my anger, my bitterness, and my lack of forgiveness,
And yet You whisper, "Be still."

You draw me into Your presence,
And speak words of grace.
Your gentleness, Your care,
And Your loving embrace,
Heal the wounds inflicted,
And covers my face;
As I sit and truly experience the gospel's grace.

Forgiveness is healing,
Your presence is healing.
I know You, God,
Everything about You is appealing.

You are the One true King,
You will return.
You call us to be ready,
And I really want to turn.
I want to turn and live,
Turn from my sin,
That holds me down,
All I have to do is forgive.

The hurt is great,
But You covered that hate.
You are with me now,
Every step that I take.

The Gospel is God's presence,
You call us to live it out.
I love You, Lord,
Help me deal with this now.

I want to walk in freedom,
Every step that I take.
Pointing people to You, Jesus,
With every breath that I take.

You forgive me Lord,
The burden is lifted.
I can live this life,
Because of Your decision.

Thank You, Lord,
For not giving up on me.
Your Gospel's grace,
Has set me free.

3. *Good Morning Abba! ~ Little Girl's prayer*

November 14, 2015

Good morning Abba! Good morning Abba!
I want to talk with You!
Good morning Abba! Good morning Abba!
I know You want to talk to me too!

I went to school yesterday,
And talked to a little girl.
She was sad and unhappy and I remembered You said,
"Go into all the world!"

You told me Abba,
To "Go into all the world and preach the gospel to men." **(Mark 16:15)**
And so I shared this truth with her,
"You have a Father in heaven."

I gave her a hug and said,
"Your Father in heaven loves you, and He wants you to be His little girl.

All you have to do is pray and receive Christ into your heart,
And you will be his most treasured pearl."

The little girl looked at me, Abba,
With huge eyes and said,
"I want Him to be my Daddy,"
And so she prayed the prayer I led.

Good morning Abba! Good morning Abba!
What do You want to tell me?
And I heard Your whispered voice saying,
"You are My Beloved daughter in whom I am well pleased."

4. Good Morning Abba! ~ Little Boy's Prayer

November 14, 2015

Good morning Abba! Good morning Abba!
Guess what?!
I caught a snake yesterday, and brought him into the house,
And my Mama screamed and fell on her butt.

Daddy walked in,
And said, "Son, what are you doin'?"
I'm not supposed to lie,
So, I said, "Daddy! Look at this snake; I caught him without a fight!"

Abba! Daddy screamed a little bit too.
But I'm not supposed to tell anyone because that's just not what guys are
supposed to do.
But Abba, the snake is really cool,
I want to keep him but Daddy and Mama said that's against their rule.

Abba! I think they made up that rule on the spot,
I don't remember them every saying that. Did they get caught?
What am I supposed to do Abba? I really like the snake.
And then I heard Your whispered voice say, "Son, listen to your parents
and obey."

5. Good Morning Abba! ~ Family Prayer

November 16, 2015

Good morning Abba! Good morning Abba!
We present ourselves to You!
As a family, we sit and pray and seek,
And wait to hear what You want us to do.

What is Your will for our family, Abba?
How do You want us to serve You?
We only want to be,
Where we will best glorify You.

Our hearts are burdened for the hurting,
Those who have suffered great loss.
For we ourselves have experienced,
Life's trials, the pain and the cost.

You comforted us with Your love,
And so, we want to comfort others.
And just remind them that,
There is a Father in heaven who loves and covers.

Our pain is only temporary,
Our eyes are set on heaven.

Where there will be no more tears,
And our hearts will be strengthened.

Thank You in advance Abba,
For the many opportunities.
To be Your hands and feet,
In the lives of the least of these.

6. Good Morning Abba! ~ Family Prayer 2

November 16, 2015

Good morning Abba! Good morning Abba!
We lift up our hands to You!
As a family, we sing and praise and worship,
Just in awe of all that You do.

Good morning Abba! Good morning Abba!
This is Billy.
Yesterday, I had a really good day!
Mommy said I was being silly.

I got a nerf gun for my birthday,
And thought I would test it out.
I sort of got Mommy in the head,
But she didn't pout.

Thank You Abba for Mommy,
I really love her a lot.
She's the best Mommy in the world,
Because she plays and sings, and taught me how to tie knots.

Abba! You are pretty awesome.
I'm in awe of how You move.
Thank You for sending Your Son, Jesus,
He lives in my heart and tells me what to do.

Good morning Abba! Good morning Abba!
This is Suzie!
My twin Billy said he had a good day yesterday,
But mine was sort of a doozie.

I really wanted to be good.
Honest I did.
But those cookies were so tempting.
So, I ate them and Daddy said, "What are you doing kid?"

And Abba, I sort of lied to Daddy,
I couldn't look him in the eye.
Please forgive me for lying like that.
Daddy sat me down and asked me "Why?"

I did tell Daddy the truth,
Those cookies were just calling my name.
I couldn't resist the temptation,
And now I'm feeling the pain.

After I got in trouble,
Daddy sat me on his lap.
We prayed and sang songs to You, Abba,
And then we took a little nap.

I'm so thankful for my Daddy, Abba.
I know he loves me a lot.
I want to marry someone like him one day,
When I'm allowed to tie the knot.

Abba! I'm so thankful for Your forgiveness,
And Jesus Christ's death on the cross.
I know I have the hope of heaven one day,
And so now I want to share the gospel with the lost.

Good morning Abba! Good morning Abba!
This is Mommy.
To be honest I'm tired from yesterday,
And I really need You to talk to me.

Confession, I locked myself in the bathroom yesterday,
While the kids were playing about.
I just needed to hear Your comforting voice,
Above all their shouts.

You reminded me that I prayed for twins.
And yes, they are a blessing.
However, Abba! I thought I specifically prayed for just one set of twins,
But that prayer must have not gotten farther than the ceiling.

Two sets of twins Abba!
This was not the plan.
Thankfully Kai and Kennedy are sleeping right now,
Next to the fan.

You told me You would give me the strength,
I'm feeling a little weary.
I'm wondering if I should ask Mom to move in,
But You said You would be with me.

I know I'm being selfish.
I do love my kids a lot.
They are all a sweet blessing from You,
And they do entertain me non-stop.

I want them to truly know Jesus,
And to go into all the world.
To preach the gospel reflecting His nature,
And to be good little boys and girls.

I'm so thankful for my Husband's wisdom and strength,
You truly blessed me with him.
He is so incredibly patient with us all,
Would You please encourage him?

Abba! Thank You for Your Word,
It is my anchor when the chaos reigns.
I love You so much, Lord,
Thank You for loving me even when I'm a pain.

Good morning Abba! Good morning Abba!
This is Dad.
I absolutely love my family Abba,
My kids think I'm pretty rad.

The twins are 5 and 2,
And they keep us on our toes.
My wife is a real trooper, though,
She is constantly on the go.

Abba! Would You comfort my wife today,
And meet her right where she is at?
I know she longs to hear Your voice and rest,
She seriously wears so many hats.

Thank You for giving me the right words with Suzie.
I can't believe my little girl lied to me.
What's it going to be like when she's a teenager, Abba,
And she asks for my keys?

Oh Abba! I need more wisdom in order to raise these kids.
I really feel like I know nothing.
Their questions get to me,
And I feel like I'm constantly researching something.

These kids are really a true blessing,
A sweet answer to prayer.
But two sets of twins, Abba,
I think I'm going to lose all of my hair.

My girls are never dating.
I've decided that already.
And if any boy comes close to them,
My fist will be ready.

My boys are really gifted,
I see Your hand on them.
Please guide me King,
So I can lead them as best that I can.

I'm so thankful for Your presence in my life.
I stand in awe as I worship You.
My heart whispers, "Come, Lord Jesus, come!"
As I lead my family in praising You.

7. One Day

November 17, 2015

I want to see You face to face, (**Revelation 22:4**)
And rest in Your warm embrace.

To worship at Your feet,
To eat at our Wedding Feast. (**Revelation 19:7-9**)

But I know it's not time,
Yet, I feel the urgency climb.

Jesus, You are coming back.
People need to realize this fact.

Fighting for souls is not easy.
But remembering all those still lost makes me queasy.

King, I need Your strength and insight,
To have impact on the battlefield and fight.

I know You are calling me to persevere in prayer,
To battle it out on my knees for the lives of Your heirs.

To stay the course,
Constantly encouraging those who suffer with remorse.

Your Word saves lives,
Penetrating hearts, protecting us from lies.

You desire us to be pure.
A lifestyle we need to ensure.

It's all about You and Your glory,
Not us, our comfort, or even our story.

Jesus, You are the key,
That unlocks the door to heaven's street.

Thank You for this life.
You've delivered me from so much strife.

You showed up each time.
I can't wait to remind,

Your people of Your power,
You are our strong tower.

One day I long to see,
And hear Your voice say that You are pleased with me.

8. *Outlast*

November 17, 2015

You told me You would never leave me or forsake me,
I'm clinging to that word right now.
I can't quite explain what is happening,
Or even how.

I'm trying to remind myself of what I know,
You're name is El Roi,
You do see everything,
That goes.

No one can hide from You,
Or cover their sin.
You will expose them,
And reveal what's within.

You care about our heart,
More than anything else.
You're calling many to repentance,
To humble themselves.

The Lord is my Helper,
I will not fear man.
Try as he might to harm me,
My God is bigger than him.

I know You have allowed this to happen.
It was all filtered through Your loving hands.
I just don't understand why,
I'm a target in their evil plan.

There is an enemy out there.
He is trying to tear down.
But we Christians need to unite and fight,
On this spiritual battleground.

I will persevere in prayer,
Lifting my fellow Christians up to You.
For that is the only way
We will win this battle—with Truth.

Uncertainty is all around me,
Wars are increasing,
There is craziness on the streets,
Lord, it feels so overwhelming.
But thank You for reminding me,
Jesus You are coming back,
You have a plan,
And You will outlast.

You will outlast all those,
Who try to come against You,
Who hurt Your saints, blaspheme Your name,
And try to get You to move.
You will outlast.

You are in my midst,
Fighting what I can't see.
Would I remember Lord Jesus,
This battle is not about me.

This battle is not against,
Flesh or blood.
Would I take myself out of it,
And truly see with eyes of Love.

Jesus, You died on the cross for all mankind,
Would the burden increase on my heart,
To go, be bold, preach the gospel,
And watch You transform their mind.

9. Submit, My Bride

November 19, 2015

I hate the thought of people listening and eavesdropping,
On my conversation with You,
As I bare my sinner heart,
And reveal what is true.
But I hear You saying,
"I want to talk to you." (**Psalm 27:8**)

I hear you saying,
"I want your love." (**John 14:15**)
That stops my wandering heart,
As I feel chased from above.

I hear You saying,
"I want you walking worthy of the call." (**Ephesians 4:1**)
But I'm struggling and failing,
And feeling beaten by all.

I feel like I'm constantly being tested,
And it's true.
I hear You saying,
"I want you to forgive the person who wronged you, (**Colossians 3:13**)
Who wronged your family member, your friend,
And not give them what's due."

I see my pride,
In all of this.
My self-righteousness,
And of course, my lack of forgiveness.

Forgive me Lord,
I do want to be,
What You called me,
And raised me to be.

You teach me Your truths,
And test me to see whether I will live the lesson.
I've failed Lord,
Will You give me a second chance, then?

I hear You saying,
"You've got it all wrong. (**Hebrews 10:10**)
It's not by perfect works,
That you run."

"It's faith in Me, (**Romans 5:8**)
That allows you to be,
The woman I've called you,
And raised you to be."

Faith endures trials, (**James 1:2**)
Understands temptations, (**James 1:12**)
Produces doers, (**James 1:22**)
And is demonstrated in separation.

Separation from the world
And obedience to You.
Faith obeys the Word.
Jesus, You are the glue.

Faith waits patiently for You!
Jesus, You are coming back!
Would I walk worthy,
And my faith not lack.

You want heroic endurance,
And a special spiritual toughness.
I hear You saying,
"I am with you in the midst of this." (**Matthew 28:20**)

So I read Your Word,
And patiently persevere in prayer; (**Isaiah 40:31**)
Baring my heart,
Knowing You Jesus are right here. (**Hebrews 13:5**)

I don't care anymore,
If they hear,
My sinner heart,
And know my fear.

My prayer is one like Paul, (**Philippians 1:12-14**)
That my prison guard,
Would hear it all.
And know You, Jesus,
Your grace and Your call.

So I fearlessly enter Your presence,
Assured of Your glad welcome. (**Ephesians 3:12**)
I love You God!
I hear You saying, "Come!"

I hear You saying, "I want your love.
Repent and live free. (**Acts 3:19**)
Preach the gospel, (**Mark 16:15**)
Wherever I place your feet.

"It's not up to you to decide, (**Jeremiah 29:11**)
Who hears the truth,
I'm speaking through your life.
Just walk worthy of My call.
Submit, My Bride."

10. Believe Me.

November 20, 2015

I don't know if I truly grasp,
Your love for me.
I'm still wondering if there is a fee.
I honestly can't repay You Lord, as You can see.
Then I hear Your whispered voice say,
"Believe Me. It's free."

What do You mean,
"No strings attached."
How can that be in this world,
Where there is always a "catch."

Then I hear Your whispered voice,
Say again,
"I love you. I've sacrificed My Son.
Believe Me. You're forgiven."

Your Words penetrate my heart.
I've fallen short,
A sinner in need of grace,
Recognizing Jesus died and took my place.

I repent of my sin Lord,
And receive Christ into my life.
As my personal Lord and Savior,
Please help me every day of my life.

Your love floods my soul,
It's something new,
But will never grow old.

You're my new Best Friend,
With so many stories,
I hear Your whispered voice say again,
"Believe Me. Our talking will never end."

I still can't believe it's free.
Your loving grace is beyond me.

I'm excited to tell my friends,
"Believe me. There is Hope,
And a loving conversation that will never end."

Thank You for Your grace, Lord.
For knowing exactly what I need.
You, Lord, know my strengths and weaknesses,
And You still love me.

11. Integrity

November 20, 2015

You keep reminding me,
That it doesn't matter what people think.
You are pleased with my integrity.

Integrity shines in the dark.
It's our character.
It's our heart.

12. A Simple Touch

November 22, 2015

What do I have to offer?
What do I have to give?
That will make an impact,
In the life they live?

What can I say?
What verse do I share?
That will make an impact,
And show them You care?

Jesus, You know,
Skid Row,
Is a place where some people glow,
As lights on Dark Row.

Some are on hard times,
Some made bad choices.
Some need to be reminded,
You, Jesus, still hear their voices.

A simple touch,
Goes such a long way.
A prayer. A hug.
Brightens their day.

Jesus, I just want to be,
Your hands and feet.
To lift the needs,
Of those who live in defeat.

You said You would be pleased,
If I gave a cup of cold water,
To the least of these.
Choosing to have,
The eyes to see,
It will meet,
Their exact need.

Thank You Lord,
For the opportunity,
To take my eyes off of myself,
And place them on Your people in need.

13. Unite and Impact

November 24, 2015

How is the church to unite,
If we don't live out Your truth,
But fight?

It's what Satan wants.
He plants seeds of strife,
So Christians fight,
And hate life.

You say happy are the peacemakers, (**Matthew 5:9**)
For they shall be called sons of God.
Do we know how to make peace,
Or only how to make fun?

Are we tearing down our brothers and sisters in Christ,
Or upholding them in prayer?
You Lord are going to have to convict our hearts,
And bring us to a point of humility and care.

Too many people leave the church over small issues.
When what we all really need to do is to humble ourselves, (**2 Chronicles 7:14**)
Forgive or ask for forgiveness, letting God change our views.

You want Your church to unite and impact,
To reach the lost,
With love and tact.

But first we need,
To live out the gospel in the family.
It starts at home,
Between you and me.

With the world looking in,
Do they want to join?
Or do they see,
A family torn?

Are you walking wise,
In your own eyes?
Not recognizing that you,
Need forgiveness too,
And a Savior to rescue you?
The conviction is great,
Forgive my hate.
They are a child of God.
I deserve Your rod.

When do people truly see Your glory,
And Your Presence show up?
Is it not when two,
Fighting Christians makeup?

Somebody has to die to them self,
And recognize the needs of another,
And help.

The world hates us,
We need each other.
That's why You commanded,
Us to love one another.

We are stronger together,
Not apart.
Would we humble ourselves, Lord,
And unite with one heart.

How are we to impact,
If we don't support each other?
It's a heart issue, Lord,
Would we humble ourselves and love our sister and brother.

Jesus, You are coming back,
And You care about Your Bride.
You want Your church walking worthy,
Uniting while they run this Christian race of life.

14. Rejoice Now

November 25, 2015

I will rejoice now,
Before the delivery.
I will rejoice now,
Before the recovery.

My battle stance is on my knees,
As I pray and seek,
The One True King.

I will rejoice now,
And not sit in defeat.
I will rejoice now,
Even if I feel beat.

My battle stance is on my knees,
As I worship to please,
My King.

I will rejoice now,
Before I see.
I will rejoice now,
Knowing You are writing my story.

My Battle stance is on my knees,
As I surrender to,
My King.

I will rejoice now,
Before the victory.
I will rejoice now,
In humility.

My battle stance is on my knees,
Honoring and glorifying,
My King.

15. *That Song*

November 25, 2015

Even when I feel defeat overwhelm me,
That song plays,
And I'm surrendered on my knees.

Crazy how a simple song,
Has so much power on a heart.
Your words to music, Lord,
Is pure art.

It captures my attention,
And pulls me out of a mood.
I'm so thankful Lord,
For those who have understood.

16. He Needed To See

November 27, 2015

Will you forgive,
Those who threw you in the fire?
Will you forgive,
Those who turned it seven times hotter?

Will you stand strong,
In your convictions?
Knowing that when God delivers you,
It impacts those who made the initial decision.
To throw you in the fire,
Turning it seven times hotter.

Maybe that was God's original plan,
To reach the hard hearted man.
Who needed to see,
Jesus walking amidst the least of these.

The world is weak,
As they conform,
To whomever out performs.

So when you stand stronger,
And people see your delivery.

They are drawn to Jesus,
Who set you free.

Will you forgive,
Those who threw you in the fire?
Will you forgive,
Those who turned it seven times hotter?

17. At Your Feet

November 27, 2015

No one understands,
My love for You.
The desire I have,
To sit at Your feet and not move.

I love You.
I love Your voice.
Your calm but firm words of truth,
Heal my choice.

I'm forgiven and free,
Because You died for me.
How can I better express my thanks,
Than giving You all of me.

You defended Mary,
When she was mocked and scorned.
For her one act of devotion, outperformed,
All of the men,
Who were specifically chosen.

With expensive perfume,
She anointed Your feet.
A true act of worship,
As she prepared You for what others called defeat.

She gave everything she had,
Knowing You gave everything for her.
A true act of worship,
Surrendered and sure.

No one understood,
Their focus was on their own.
But You Jesus defended Mary,
And said, "Leave her alone."

No one understands,
My love for You.
To pray and intercede,
For those You choose.

But I rest assured,
Knowing You will defend me.
As I sit and pray,
At Your feet.

18. I Know You, God!

November 27, 2015

I know You, God! (**Jeremiah 9:24**)
I know You.

You said You would,
Work this out for my good. (**Romans 8:28**)
Even as that meant, this issue would,
Conform me more into Christ's image. (**Romans 8:29**)
I understood.

You told me to trust You.
To not lean on my own understanding,
But to acknowledge You.
And You would direct my path in everything! (**Proverbs 3:5-6**)

You told me to forgive,
As Christ has forgiven me. (**Colossians 3:15**)
Laying down His life,
Setting me free.

Will I do the same?
For those who hurt me?
Or hold them in bondage,
Refusing to set them free?

I know You, God!
I know You!

You told me that You have not
Given me a spirit of fear.
But of power, love and a sound mind, (**2 Timothy 1:7**)
To encourage my peers.

You told me You are,
The God of peace.
And shortly You would,
Crush Satan under Your feet. (**Romans 16:20**)

You told me to be steadfast and immoveable.
Always abounding in Your work,

Knowing that my labor is not in vain, (**1 Corinthians 15:58**)
And You see my hard work.

You told me vengeance is Yours.
You will repay evil for evil. (**Romans 12:19**)
I'm just to sit back and pray,
And let You deal with all this upheaval.

I know You, God!
I know You!

You told me to hang out with the humble. (**Romans 12:16**)
To bless those who persecute me. (**Romans 12:14**)
To help other Christians, (**Romans 12:13**)
And to grow in hospitality. (**Romans 12:13**)

You told me to rejoice in hope.
To be patient in tribulation.
To continue steadfastly in prayer; (**Romans 12:12**)
And to be kind to other brothers and sisters and honor them. (**Romans 12:10**)

You told me that love never gives up!
It never loses faith.
It is always hopeful,
Enduring through every circumstance and trial in this race. (**1 Corinthians 13:7**)

You told me to pray and not worry.
Your peace would guard my mind. (**Philippians 4:6-7**)
I'm taking up Your helmet of salvation, Lord, (**Ephesians 6:17**)
Protecting what's mine.

I know You, God!
I know You.

My foundation is firm.
I've entrusted my life to You.
And I know You will return.

19. Revival

November 27, 2015

Repentance is the match,
That sparks the flame,
Of revival deep within.

It starts with us.
Our personal walk.
Are we praying and seeking,
Or is it all just talk?

Where is our heart,
Is it cold and hardened?
Are we walking through this life,
Bored and heavy laden?

If we are not repenting,
We won't hear God's voice.
So when we are met with a decision,
We won't make the right choice.

Repentance is the match,
That sparks the flame,
Of revival deep within.

As we repent we see,
Our burdens flee.
Recognizing the Man, who took it all,
While nailed to that tree.

The freedom it brings,
Revives the cold heart.
Bringing life to the surface,
Sparking a flame that lights the dark.

Repentance is the match,
That sparks the flame,
Of revival deep within.
One heart on fire,
Sparks another.
And revival spreads to all the men.

20. Send Me

November 28, 2015

Christian, God has placed you right where you are,
For such a time as this.
God has given you this position for a reason,
So take a risk.

Vision often starts,
With a broken heart.
What are you seeing and hearing right now,
That is tearing you apart?

Could that not be God's voice,
Shouting above the noise?
Trying to get someone's attention,
To step up and make a choice.

A choice that can change a life,
For the better.
How long has God been calling out,
But no one's read His letter.

Lord, forgive me for being deaf,
To Your voice.
There are those still hurting,
Because I failed to make that choice.

The very thing that breaks my heart,
Should have opened my eyes and my ears.
To Your voice crying out,
Saying, "Who will go for Me and rescue my heirs?"

"Send Me, Lord, and strengthen my hands,
To do Your will.
And accomplish the work,
For Your honor and glory, not my thrill."

This life is not about me.
Have I not realized that yet?
Why am I blind
To all the needs that have not been met?

You have a plan,
And it is good.
Would I say, "Yes, Lord" more often,
To Your voice, crying out above the noise in the room.

Christian, God has placed us right where we are,
For such a time as this.
God has given us this position for a reason,
So let's take a risk.

Vision often starts,
With a broken heart.
What are we seeing and hearing right now,
That is tearing us apart?

Will we hear Your voice and pray,
And take that step of faith today?
Jesus, You hold the key,
"Send Me!"

21. John 21

December 1, 2015

I failed again.
The guilt is deep.
The burden is so heavy.
I'm struggling with defeat.

I returned to what I know.
I didn't know what else to do.
Then everybody followed,
And we stopped doing what You called us to.

Then You showed up.
And asked if we had any food.

We answered you, "No."
And You told us what You wanted us to do.

After toiling all night,
We listened to Your words of advice,
And tossed our net to the other side,
Realizing we were not as wise.

"It is the Lord," said John.
So as we pulled in multitudes of fish,
I dove into the throng,
And swam to shore towards Jesus.

"Come and eat breakfast," You said.
And so we sat down with You,
And ate until we all were fed.

"Simon, son of Jonah, do you love
Me more than these?"
I heard Your voice so clearly,
Trembling on my knees.

"Yes, Lord; You know that I love You."
I responded in defeat.
Remembering what I had previously done,
Not wanting to boast, but admit, I'm weak.

He said to me,
"Feed My lambs."
Did I hear him correctly?
I'm an unrighteous man.

And then He said to me again,
"Simon, son of Jonah, do you love Me?"
He's looking straight at me,
I want to flee.

But staying under His gaze,
I responded on cue.
"Yes Lord;
You know that I love You."

He then said to me,
"Tend my sheep."
Tend His sheep?
I'm about to weep.

But He didn't stop there, a third time He asked,
"Simon, son of Jonah, do you love Me?"
My face, I can't mask!
My heart is grieving.

And I responded at last,
"Lord, You know all things;
You know that I love You."
Oh, what else do I say to my King?

I can't believe,
I've struggled so badly.
This is my King,
And He is looking at me so tenderly.
"Feed My sheep," He said.
Again, He's giving me an opportunity,
When I don't deserve,
To feed the least of these.

But Jesus didn't stop there, He continued and said,
"When you were younger, you walked wherever you wished.
But know this, when you are older,
Your hands will be stretched out and another will carry you where you do
not wish."

What does this mean?
This word spoken from the Man
Who hung on the tree.
Is He telling me,
How I will be?

But then those sweet words,
Came to my ears.
Jesus said, "Follow me."
I heard Him so clear.

What love displayed,
My heart is so relieved.
My King has forgiven,
And He re-commissioned me.

22. Waiting For Your Return

December 2, 2015

I want to be a learner,
In the school of prayer.
Lord, please make my ears deaf to the whisper,
"What's the use? No one's there."

I know You are here.
I know it.
And I know You hear.
As I pour out my heart, bit by bit.

I don't have it down.
I don't always know what to say.

So I read Your scriptures,
And pray that way.

The power is found in Your Word,
Not my voice.
As You open my eyes to scriptures,
All I can do is rejoice.
I rejoice before the answer is given.
Because You, God, are good,
And You have already freely given,
Your Son who truly understood.

I honestly don't quite understand it all.
But my heart is drawn to You, King,
And so I have to call.

I have to call on You,
Night and day.
I need to hear Your voice,
As I pray.

You're the Bridegroom
Calling out to Your Bride,
"Wake up! I'm coming. (**Romans 13:11**)
Live purely in this life." (**2 Peter 3:14**)

And I hear You, Lord,
I do.
So, I spend more time in Your presence,
Feeding on Your Word.
Interceding and praying for others,
Waiting for Your return.

23. *Come On In*

December 6, 2015

Do we weep, (**John 20:11**)
When You don't show?
Do we even ask,
"Where did He go?" (**John 20:13**)

Do we even notice,
If You are not in our midst?
Or are we preoccupied
With our own list.

Forgive us Lord.
Please search our hearts and minds.
Point out anything that offends You,
And help us to be of one mind.

Would we see,
That church is not about "me."
It's about You,
Magnified in honor right through eternity.

We do long for Your glory
In our midst.
We seriously just want to be,
In Your Presence.

Forgive our hard hearts, Lord.
Search us and find,
Anything amiss.
Please help us to be kind.

You alone get the glory,
Our gifts are to honor You.
Forgive us Lord,
If we've taken something that belongs to You.

Do we weep, (**John 20:11**)
When You don't show?
Do we even ask,
"Where did He go?" (**John 20:13**)

Do we even notice,
If You are not in our midst?
Or are we preoccupied,
With our own list.

We repent of our sin, Lord.
And turn back to You.
Please receive all honor and praise,
And not give us what is due.

We need You to show up,
In Your house, Lord.
We desperately need You,
We were created for You. (**Revelation 4:11**)

It is by Your will that we exist,
We are most complete worshiping like this.

Lord, we just want,
To be where You are.
So send us to that place.
Is it far?

Or are You right here,
Just waiting to be invited in.
Forgive us again Lord.
Please come on in. (**Revelation 3:20**)

24. Life In Jesus' Name

December 7, 2015

God turns scars into stars,
As you relinquish control;
Letting Him mold you more into Christ's image, (**Romans 8:29**)
Who bore scars for the world.

A scar tells a story,
It adds character to life.
God never promised it would be easy,
But He did say He would guide us through it with His eye. (**Psalm 32:8**)

Nail pierced hands,
Were scarred for us.
Giving us the hope of heaven,
And eternal life face to face with Jesus.

On the cross His perfect form took our sin and shame,
Scarred for all mankind,
Declaring forever,
There is life in Jesus' name.

Jesus' scars tell a story,
Of God redeeming mankind.
The pain He endured,
Was so that we could find,
Life in Jesus' name.

God turns scars into stars,
As you relinquish control,
Letting Him mold you more into Christ's image,
Who bore scars for the world.

Your scar tells a story,
Of how God redeemed you,
From life's trials and hardships,
And healed you through and through.

The scar remains,
To tell a story;
A story that says,
There is Life in Jesus' name.

God turns scars into stars,
Because stars shine in the dark,
Lighting the way;
For those following to see,
There is life in Jesus' name.

25. A Great Light

December 9, 2015

A light shined, (**Isaiah 9:2**)
Did you see it?
It's been so dark lately,
But something was lit.

We've been walking in fear,
Trying to hide from the chaos all around,
But a great light shined,
And we were found.

We were found inadequate,
In need of a Savior.

Someone to rescue us,
From this fear.

Did you see,
The great light shine?
It didn't condemn,
But invited us in.

Welcoming us with grace,
Declaring a Savior,
Is born,
The Prince of Peace.

I want to know this Savior,
This Great High Priest
Who sympathizes,
And knows I'm just one of the least.

I want to know Him
And make Him known.
Encouraging people to be reconciled,
And stand strong in the light shone.

26. The Fire

December 10, 2015

When you're in the fire,
You're more on fire.
There's something about the burn,
That makes your heart turn.

It turns toward Christ,
And clings to the promises found in the Word of Life.

Walking confidently, sustained,
By Christ through all the pain.

There's something about opposition,
That reminds me of competition.

When Satan wants me to quit,
Jesus Christ is more on my lips.

Look around you,
Who's boldly sharing Christ with no crew.

Who's blazing a trail,
While others bail.

Bailing out on key opportunities,
To impact the least of these.

The person on fire,
Is in the fire.

Not backing down.
Taking ground.

Blazing a trail.
Passing others too afraid to fail.

If it's going to take being in the fire,
For you to be on fire.

My prayer is that you'll feel the heat.
So that you finally hit the street.

Jesus Christ is coming back.
He doesn't want you trailing the pack.

This life is not about you.
Stop holding onto the Words of life,
God has shared with you.

And share Christ's love,
With those needing a word from above.

It's time to wake up and see,
Our salvation is nearer now than when we first believed. (**Romans 13:11**)

27. I'm Not Alone

December 12, 2015

The cross was Jesus' mission,
His heart displayed.
Turning rejection into redemption,
Love fully paid.

Redeeming rejected mankind,
Restoring broken lives.
Healing the hurting at the perfect time.

Dying a cruel torturous death,
Ascending to heaven into God's presence.
His love gave us life after death.

I know that my Redeemer lives.
He's seated on the throne.

Interceding and loving me,
Reminding me that by God's grace, I'm not alone.

I walk through life with Him by my side.
I'm protected in His presence.
Confident to go and multiply.

Sharing, "We've all fallen short,
Sinners in need of grace,
Please recognize there is a Savior,
That died and took our place."

"If you repent of your sin,
And receive Jesus Christ into your life,
As your personal Lord and Savior,
You're guaranteed eternal life,
In heaven with Him,
Free from every burden you carry within."

28. The Greatest Gift

December 13, 2015

Glory to God,
He's healed my heart.
Given me the gift of heaven,
So now I'm ready to start,
Living this life,
As He called me to.
Sharing the gospel,
Even though I'm new.

I don't know much,
But I'm willing to go.
Jesus please give me the right words,
So I'm ready if they want to know.

The truth of the risen King,
Jesus Christ is our everything.
Born in a manger, a perfect man,
Dying a horrible death was all a part of God's plan.

Glory to God,
My soul magnifies the Lord.
He's given me this sweet gift,
So I'm ready to be poured.

Poured out for all mankind,
Sharing Christ's truths.
So people will find,
The greatest gift, the King of the Jews.

29. Lord Jesus, I Need You

December 17, 2015

Lord, I need to hear Your voice,
Whisper softly to my heart.
I need to feel Your presence,
Like a warm hug, guarding me from the dark.

You are all I need.
I long for You.

You are everything to me.
Lord Jesus, I need You.

Lord, I need to see with Your eyes,
All those hurting around me.
I think I've been really blind,
To the needs You've been trying to show me.

You are all they need.
Would they see that?
You are the answer to everything.
Lord Jesus, would they realize that?

I need to pray according to Your will,
Lifting up those You've burdened my heart.
As a fellow Christian,
Fighting the dark.

Lord, I don't understand what is happening,
But I trust that You know everything.
So I lean into Your warm embrace,
As You guard and protect me from the things I'm called to face.

With You by my side I can face it.
No fear on my heart,
I've surrendered it.
You, Lord Jesus, have conquered it.

You are all I need.
I long for You.
You are everything to me.
Lord Jesus, I need You.

30. *Your Word*

December 18, 2015

I want to sit here,
Just a little bit longer.
Until Your Word,
Becomes even more clearer.

31. *Don't Panic*

December 19, 2015

Don't panic.
Don't be troubled.
Do not fear.
For I AM here.

I Am with you,
Every step of the way.
Do not fear.
This trial will not stay.

Keep your eyes on Me.
I will see you through.
I AM holding your hand.
Leading you.

I have overcome the world.
Satan will not win.
Trust me, children.
This will work out in the end.

32. Teach Me to Love Like You

December 20, 2015

I love You, Lord.
I do.
Please teach me to love,
Like You.

Lord, I don't want to hurt her.
I just don't understand.
We're engaged to be married,
Why would she choose another man?

And then an angel of the Lord,
Met me in a dream,
And said, "Joseph, son of David,
It's not what it seems.

Do not be afraid to take Mary as your wife,
For the child she carries,
God has given life.

She will have a son,
And you are to name him Jesus.
He will be the Savior for mankind,
Immanuel, God with us!"

I love You, Lord.
I do.
Please teach me to love,
Like You.

Thank you Lord for assuring my heart,
The love of my life,
Has remained faithful from the start.

I don't know why You've chosen me,
To be the earthly father,
Of the child that will be,
One day nailed to a tree.

But, Lord, I promise to love,
This little boy like my own.
I will cherish the days,
And teach him what I know.

Thank you Lord for choosing me,
To be the man this little boy needs.
It's a blessing from above,
To love this little child that is not my own flesh and blood.

I love You, Lord.
I do.
Thank you for teaching me to love,
Like You.

33. O God You Are My God

Psalm 63:1-4
December 21, 2015

O God, You are my God,
I will seek You.
O God, You are my God,
I long for You.

I look for You in the sanctuary.
Hoping You will show.
I long to see Your glory.
Your power and presence that glows.

Your lovingkindness overwhelms my soul.
It is better than life.
It will never grow old.

My lips shall praise You
As long as I live.
I will lift up my hands,
And extol the name who gives.

Life.
Beyond the grave.
Life.
For eternity. He saves!

O God, You are my God,
I will seek You.
O God, You are my God,
I long for You.

I will bless You while I live.
I will rejoice and sing,
To the One who gives.

Life.
Beyond the grave.
Life.
For eternity. He saves!

34. I Know You Love Me

December 26, 2015

I know You love me, Lord.
You remind me every day.
I know You love me, Lord.
You get creative in how you say:

"I love you.
You are Mine.
I will always love you.
For all time."

Nothing will ever separate me from Your love,
No height nor depth,
Nor any created thing from above,
Will come in between this love.

No person, trial, distress or persecution,
Shall ever separate me from this Person,
Sent from above,
The Man who died for love.

No famine, nakedness, peril or sword,
Shall ever come between me and the love of my Lord.
I am a conqueror in Christ,
Because of Love, who paid the ultimate price.

Nailed to a tree,
This Man died for me.
Taking my place,
Before I even said 'Yes' to His face.

Showing true love,
Is sent from above.
A gift of God's grace,
Pleading my case,
Taking my place,
Saying, "She is free from this disgrace."

I know You love me, Lord.
You remind me every day.
I know You love me, Lord.
You get creative in how you say:

"I love you.
You are Mine.
I will always love you.
For all time."

35. Forgive Me Lord

December 26, 2015

Forgive me Lord,
Again and again,
Forgive me.

Forgive me Lord,
Again and again,
Forgive me.

I long to do something good,
I want to do something great.

But I get stuck in the past,
Remembering all my mistakes.

I want to move forward,
But I feel bound in chains.
Like a prisoner chained to a guard,
Remembering all the previous pain.

Forgive me Lord,
Again and again,
Forgive me.

Forgive me Lord,
Again and again,
Forgive me.

I know You have a plan,
But my feet are dragging.
Why can't I let go,
And run this race without lagging.

Why is my memory so good?
Remembering all those who misunderstood.
When I had already forgiven,
Those who placed me in this position.

I want to think rightly,
So please take away these thoughts.
Change my perspective, Lord,
So I can run this race as I ought.

Forgive me Lord,
Again and again,
Forgive me.

Forgive me Lord,
Again and again,
Forgive me.

I want to be more like Christ,
Seeking the lost,
Impacting their life,

With the truth of God's grace,
Encouraging them to run this race,
With their eyes on Christ,
Not the past, the pain, or the vice,
That wants to hold them down,
Keeping them bound,
In the chains called, "Me,"
When Jesus Christ has already set them free.

It's not about me,
It's not about them.
These self-centered chains,
Keep us from the end.

Forgive us Lord,
Again and again,
Forgive us.

Forgive us Lord,
Again and again,
Forgive us.

Thank You for Your grace.
It's the only way I can run this race.
Taking my thoughts captive,
Using the past to give,
Encouragement to those struggling,
And a word on forgiving.

It's a lesson from above,
One we all need to learn to love.
And to live it out,
Knowing Christ is coming back, without a shadow of a doubt.

Forgive us Lord,
Again and again,
Forgive us.

Forgive us Lord,
Again and again,
Forgive us.

36. Victory

Revelation 1

Is this real?
Could this be?
Jesus, My King?

Am I seeing what I think?
My resurrected King?

It's been so long.
The pain has been great.
I don't know why I'm here,
Isolated and alone because of hate.

There is no fear in love. (**1 John 4:18**)
Perfect love casts out fear.

I know this comes from above,
Jesus, I know You hear.

I love You, (**1 John 4:19**)
Because You first loved me.
Your love was displayed,
On that tree.

And now I hear behind me a voice,
Saying, "I am the Alpha and the Omega, (**Revelation 1:11**)
The First and the Last.
Write what you see in a book,
And send it to the churches I've asked."

Is this real?
Could this be?
Jesus, My King?

Am I seeing what I think?
My resurrected King?

And when I truly saw Him, (**Revelation 1:17**)
I fell at His feet as dead.
He laid His right hand on me,
And said,

"Do not be afraid; (**Revelation 1:17**)
For I am the First and the Last.
I am He who lives, (**Revelation 1:18**)
And was dead,

And behold,
I am alive forevermore."
This Revelation is true,
Jesus has opened a door.

For the time is near,
For Christ's return.
Do not fear,
It's Victory's turn.

37. Wrestling

I'm wrestling.
I'm struggling.
I'm not sure if I'm listening.
This battle is waging,
My heart is raging.

I keep going,
Back and forth,
"Which door?"

Is it pride or confidence,
That says, "I can do this."

I can't say.
I honestly don't know,
What's in my heart today.

My heart is deceitful
And desperately wicked.
I need You, Lord.
This is over my head.

Search me, O God, (**Psalm 139:23-24**)
And know my heart.
Test me and know my thoughts.

Please reveal my part,
And show me where to start.

I want to be right before You.
I hate sin.
I'm so confused.

I want to be humble.
I do.
But I find I think so much about myself,
And not enough about You.

Humility is not thinking less of yourself.
It's not thinking about yourself.

Forgive me.
My prayers have been all about me.

I see how I can make a change.
There are things that are wrong.
People are suffering.

You've burdened my heart.
What's my part?

How can I impact,
And speak with tact?
So those suffering,
Will be rescued and redeemed.

You've given me gifts,
To honor and glorify You.
I need Your help, Lord,
Please show me what to do.

Is it pride or confidence,
That says, "I can do this?"

Lord, honest heart,
I believe it's confidence.

38. New

January 11, 2016

I want to smile,
But my heart is shaking.
I need a breakthrough.
Please take this King.
I've failed and I've been hurt.
It's a little bit of both.
Please tell me my worth.

I feel so small.
Taken advantage of,
And yet overlooked by all.
Failing to forgive,
And move on and live,
This life of grace,
Confident and bold in the race.

What's my identity?
What is the key?
How do I deal with all of this animosity?

If Corrie ten Boom could stick out her hand,
And forgive the man,

That killed her family.
Why can't I forgive my enemy?

Do I practice what I preach?
Or is this just a speech?
Is my smile sincere?
Or am I just hiding my fear?

Can I genuinely relinquish control?
Knowing You Lord have it all.

I know You love me.
I know You love me.
I know You love me.

You're the Father who gave up His Son,
To redeem the unloveable ones.
Because You truly cared,
What happened to all Your heirs.

My identity is in Christ.
I will stand strong and believe that in this life.
Satan is just trying to mess with my head,
To stop me from moving ahead.
I will forgive,
Because that is the only way to live.
I will ask for forgiveness,
Because that releases,
The guilt and shame,
That comes from failing in this game.

I want the freedom it brings,
So I surrender to my King.
And receive His love,
A gift from above.
Sharing that love,
As a wise steward does.

Living out the Word,
So others are stirred.
Knowing Jesus is the key,
And one day He's coming back for me.

Your Word is Your plan.
And repentance and grace,
Makes me a new man.

39. Walk Worthy

Ephesians 4
January 12, 2016

Walk worthy.
What does that mean?
How do I honor and respect,
My King?

I'm a prisoner in chains,
Bound to a man,
For preaching Christ's name.

And so I urge you,
With love.
Walk worthy of the call,
Because God has called you from above.

Be humble and gentle.
Patient with each other,
While making allowances for your brother.
He's just a man,
Needing to see Christ's love in action.

Always keep yourselves united in the Holy Spirit,
And bind yourselves together with peace.
Remembering that one day all of these people,
Will eat with you at The Wedding Feast.
We are one body, and the same Spirit,
And we've been called to the same glorious future.
So let's live like it.
There is only one Lord, one faith, one baptism,
One God and Father of all, who is above all,
And through all and in you all—it's His mission.

He's given each one of us a special gift.
He's so generous, He wants us to live.
Walking worthy of His call,
Honoring and respecting the King of all.

That is why He says,
"When He ascended to the heights, (**Ephesians 4:8**)
He led a crowd of captives
And gave gifts to His people."
And so now we can live,
This life the way He's called us to,
Knowing that grace has been given,
To all, not just a few.

He gave gifts to the church,
So they would be built up in love.
These gifts are not for ourselves,
They are to shine Christ's love from above.

How will they know we are disciples of Christ?
Our love for one another,
Pays the price,
And shines the light.

Some are apostles,
Others are prophets,
Some are evangelists,
Pastors,
And teachers.

Their responsibility is to equip God's people,
And build up the church,
The body of Christ, not just the steeple.

We are to be built up,
Until we are unified in faith,
Growing together,
Knowing God's Son,
Ready to go and share Christ's love in this race.

God doesn't want us like children,
Going back and forth,
Forever changing our minds,
Unable to discern the worth.

Of what we believe,
Nor live like the ungodly,
Who are hopelessly confused and in need.

Their minds are full of darkness.
Their hearts are hardened to the Lord.
They don't care about right or wrong,
And their immoral lives are filled with impurity and greed,
Always wanting more.

But that isn't what you were taught,
When you learned about Christ.
You've heard about Him and have learned the truth.
So throw off your old evil nature and your former way of life.
Which is rotten through and through.

There must be a spiritual renewal,
In your thoughts and attitudes.
You must display a new nature,
Because you are a new person created in God's likeness,
As righteous, holy and true.

So put away falsehood,
And tell your neighbor the truth.
Because we belong to each other,
We need to guard our bad attitudes.

Watch your anger.
Don't steal.
Use your hands for honest work,
And give generously to those who need a meal.

Don't use foul language.
But let your words be encouraging, imparting grace to the hearers.
Don't bring sorrow to God's Holy Spirit by the way you live,
Remembering His Word.

He's identified you as His own,
Your place in heaven is guaranteed.
He wants you living in freedom,
Not bound by unnecessary things.

Get rid of all bitterness, rage, anger, harsh words and slander,
As well as all types of malicious behavior.
Instead be kind to each other, tender hearted and forgiving,
Just as God forgave you, through Christ
Walk worthy, honoring and respecting your King.

40. In My Eyes

January 14, 2016

I love you,
Just the way you are.
But I want you to,
Experience the beauty of change,
Because that will take you far.

I love transforming hearts,
With the truth of My Word.
Watching people go from death to life,
As they learn.

Like a Father,
With a twinkle in His eye.
I watch you.
Like a spy.

Because I love you so much.
I want you to excel.
So I keep an eye,
Making sure you are doing well.

I want you more like Christ.
That is why I have allowed this trial in your life.
I know you.
I love you.
I am with you.
Don't worry, I will see you through.

Trust me with this.
I love you regardless.
I love you like I love My Son.

Believe Me.
In My eyes, you have already won.

41. Prayer

Prayer.
A universal language.
A heart written on a page.
A cry for help.
Love spoken to the One who hears well.
Intercession for the needy and poor.
Arrows aimed at heaven's door.

Prayer.
Brings a breath of fresh air.
A heart aligned with the King,
Interceding and bringing
Burdens and needs,
As the Throne Room's key.

42. Worth the Cost

I want your love.
Don't give it to anyone else. (**Book of Hosea**)
Seek Me first,
And I will give you everything else. (**Matthew 6:33**)

I want your heart.
Guard it from the enemy's darts.

For it affects everything you do, (**Proverbs 4:23**)
Please stay true.

I want your mind.
Come and let us reason together. (**Isaiah 1:18**)
I want to challenge you.
So let's sit and talk with one another.

I want your thoughts.
Because they affect your emotions.
So, think upon things that are noble and just, pure, lovely and good.
(**Philippians 4:8**)
Things that are contrary to the world's promotions.

I want your body.
It is the temple of the Lord. (**1 Corinthians 6:18-20**)
Don't just give that thing away,
But save it for your spouse, when I open that door.

I want your eyes.
The things they see, remain.
Look away quickly, (**Job 31:1**)
So what you see does not leave a stain.

I want your hands.
To reach out to the lost.
And serve the orphans, the widows, and the poor. (**James 1:27**)
No matter the cost.

I want your feet.
To blaze a trail,
With the gospel of peace. (**Ephesians 6:15**)
So, move forward confidently.
I have given you everything you need

I want all of you.
For I have redeemed you in the face of the lost.
Believe Me.
You are worth the cost.

43. *Silence*

Your silence serves a purpose.
I will trust You with this.
I will not stop praying.
Knowing You hear me regardless.

I will wait.
I'm working on patience.
I really want to hear Your voice.
But I know Your silence serves a purpose.

It is beautiful.
Your silence.
Something I have come to learn to love,
Knowing it is truly a gift from above.

I would like to hear Your voice.
I know I am right before You.
But Your silence reveals Your choice,
To grow me through and through.

The one who experiences Your silence,
And sees the beauty in it,
Grows more and more into Christ's image,
As they accept the honor that comes with it.

Thank You for Your love displayed,
In this silence, I'm experiencing today.
I wouldn't trade it for an explanation,
For I know it's Your highest commendation.

44. Stand In The Face Of Your Critics

As you stand in the face of your critics,
They will see Me standing with you in this.
For you listened to My voice.
You are the one who made the right choice.

I will not leave you,
Nor will I forsake you.
I Am with you.
For I have chosen you.

I do call you to take steps of faith.
Crazy steps that demand crazy faith.
Because I am moving forward with the end in sight,
Desiring ambassadors to step up and fight.

To fight for the lost.
Not content with the few.
Chasing after the wandering,
Proclaiming the Good News.

Jesus Christ saves!
I've sent My Son.
To die for their name,
To redeem the unlovable ones.

I see your works.
I know your heart.
Don't give up.
Just do your part.

I will give you a crown.
For winning souls.
The crown of rejoicing, (**1 Thessalonians 2:19**)
Is your goal.

Yes! The fruit of the righteous is life,
And he who wins souls is wise. (**Proverbs 11:30**)
I've given you this gift,
And I'm standing by your side.

As you stand in the face of your critics,
They will see Me standing with you, in this.
For you listened to My voice.
You are the one who made the right choice.

45. Gift of Life

What is my goal?
In this life You have given me.
But to share the gospel with the lost,
And use these gifts for Your glory.

My focus needs to remain on You,
As I grow in these gifts.
While trying to figure out what to do,
With this life when there is so much to choose.

I want to make the right choice.
I don't want to compare.
Comparing only brings despair,
As I fail to measure up to all Your heirs.

There are a lot of gifted people.
So many set a part.
My job is not to compare,
But to find those hidden stars.

Faithfulness is the key.
You can teach almost every other part.
But faithfulness comes from within,
It's an authentic loyal heart.

"Who can find a faithful man?" (Proverbs 20:6)
Someone loyal to the Lord and his friend.
Are they still around,
Or is corruptness only to be found?

Faithfulness refuses to lie.
It's loyalty remains to the Lord first.
Knowing God's heart and mind,
Desiring to live out His Word immersed.

In the truth of God's love.
Understanding God's words protect,
Everyone He loves,
That is why we need to live them out without defiance.

Faithfulness sets people apart.
Because their focus is God's glory,
With an authentic loyal heart,
Not their own story.

Too many want to be in the light,
When You Lord Jesus,
Are to be the only One shining bright.

It's a matter of the heart.
And You see those fighting to keep Your name set apart.
You are the Redeemer, the Savior of Mankind.
You see those using their gifts to impact the lost's mind.

What do You want me to do,
With this gift of life?
Here I am Lord,
My heart, soul and my mind.

46. The Extra Mile

Will you go the extra mile?
And not be content with the norm.
But humble yourself and serve others,
Regardless of the storm.

47. Your Path

Psalm 16:11

Your path is best.
Light it up,
And make the rest,
Dark to my eyes,

So I'm blind,
To the enemies lies.

Your presence heals.
Every hurt disappears,
As I surrender and kneel,
At Your feet,
Experiencing the fullness of joy,
That meets,
My every need.

At Your right hand is Jesus.
My Savior, my Friend.
The All-Sufficient One.
The gift that has no end.

48. Liberty

The power of Your presence protects,
Me from what I cannot control.
I know You are on my side Lord,
Because You keep reminding me there will be a reward.

The only thing I want is a crown.
So that I can cast it back at Your feet,
As I bow down.
Rejoicing for the many lives saved,
Now experiencing the freedom,
From the oppression that gave,
Them the scars they wear.
But Praise God, liberty is here.

49. Tact

Tact.
How do I share this,
Without them feeling attacked?

But I need to tell them the truth,
In love,
So that they will move,
In the direction shining from above.

Tact.
Telling the truth in such a way,
That the person appreciates your care,
And that you were not swayed,
By the world's way.

50. My Best Rest

Thank You, Lord, for this time.
It's a treasure to my heart,
Far surpassing any kind,
Of play time.

You know my best rest,
Comes from sitting in Your presence.
This is how I rest.
I talk to You.
I listen, too.

But it's the assurance,
You give,
The love of Your presence,
That lives,
Inside of my heart,
Encouraging me to simply do my part.

The stress release,
As I am free,
From the burdens that increase,
With each day.
The constant to do list,
That never sways.

As I sit and listen,
To Your awesome voice.
Encouraging my heart,
To make the choice,
To step it up,
And continue each day,
Living for Your glory,
Without delay.

So my best rest,
Comes from sitting in Your presence.
As I talk to You,
Sharing my heart,
And hearing You,
Saying, "Don't worry.
You're doing good right where you are."

51. Words Hurt

People talk,
And tear down.
Missing the fact,
That Jesus is around.

They gossip about their friend.
Even in church they tell tales,
That seem to never end.

And the hurt it brings,
To the one suffering,
Leaves scars only Jesus can heal,
As they kneel,
In His presence surrendering control,
To the One who holds,
The world.

Wounds inflicted by the tongue,
Can only be healed,
By words from the Stronger One.
Jesus our King,
Whose words remain all powerful,
Alleviating all suffering.

Words hurt.
They remain.
We remember them forever.
It's really hard to remove that stain.

When we don't control our words,
They destroy our friends.
One slip of the tongue,
And everything can end.

Why are we so mean?
What's the point?
In the church that is supposed to bring,
Freedom and comfort to the suffering.

It makes us look like the world,
When we are supposed to be set apart.
But it's our own actions, church,
That has wrecked their heart.

Who will own up to their sin, today?
And admit they have torn someone down,
With their words,
Missing the fact that Jesus is around.

He hears every word.
We will be held accountable with what we say.
Are you ready to stand before the Lord,
Seeing the scars that paid?

Forgive us Lord,
We've let You down.
As we're found,
Guilty as charged,
Spreading gossip at large.

We've hurt other people.
The depth of their scars,
We don't know.
Forgive us Lord,
And help us to show,
Love to one another,
By redeeming our sister and brother.

52. He Came to Restore

He came to restore our soul,
To give life, liberty,
And freedom from the toll,
Of the sin that brings,
Separation from our King.

53. God Knew

God knew today would happen.
It's in the book.
He's ready for your call,
Don't worry, you're not overlooked.

He wants you close.
He's actually right here.
Do you sense His presence?
Have your tears cleared?

It's ok to cry.
He knows the pain,
That constricts your heart tonight.

54. Life is Beautiful

February 16, 2016

But above all Lord, I want Your will.
Your will, Lord, in my life,
Has made life beautiful.
Your will, includes Your "yes'" and Your "no's,"
I thank You Lord because I honestly just did not know.
But You did.
And Your will proved,
To be the BEST.
And so I thank You Lord because it's allowed me to rest,
In Your sweet arms,
Safe and secure from harm,
That would have come,
Had I not listened to Your warnings,
As I sat before You every morning.

There is a reason for Your "no's,"
Would I simply listen and trust You,
When you say, "This is a No-go."
You have Your reason,
I don't always see.
But would I thank You Lord in advance?
Because You know what the best is for me.

I will wait for the best.
Why settle for less?
In this life You have given me,
This beautiful life that allows me to run free.
Not chained to a guard,
Like a prisoner falsely charged.
But running free,
Loved by the One who absolutely trusts me.

That sweet gift of trust,
I value so much,
A gift from You Lord,
It's Your will, and it's struck a chord.

Your will, Lord, in my life.
Has made my life beautiful.
People miss the reason why.
But seriously, it's because my joy bucket is full.

Filled to the brim,
From sitting in Your presence,
Rejoicing and singing sweet hymns,
Experiencing true joy in absolute fullness.

Your "yes'" in my life,
Are like smiles from on High.
A shining of Your face,
In my direction makes my heart race.
As I see You open the door,
A gentleman to the core.
Showing me,
The life that will be,
So beautiful,
Because You care about my soul.

55. Your Voice

February 19, 2016

Lord, I want so desperately to hear Your voice,
Because I really need to make the right choice.

I want to hear what You are telling me, not the crowd.
So, I listen to You, Lord, not what is loud.

Your still small voice I long to hear.
So I know how to handle this situation that is so dear.
Everyone has an opinion.
But I don't care what they think.
I will not decide based on the popular decision.
For their way always has a missing link.

You know all things.
I want Your will.
Please speak Lord,
Your servant listens.
I want to obey Your voice.
So right now, I'm being still.

56. Forever. And. A. Day.

February 20, 2016

Forever. And. A. Day.
You are worth the wait.
I've been praying for you every day,
Wondering about our first date.

I just want to talk to you.
A simple conversation.
Please do not call me "boo,"
I've never liked that nick-name.

It fits some people.

But it doesn't fit me.
I'm kind of an old soul,
Simple is the key.

God promised me,
You'd be a man after His own heart.
Believe me,
He was right from the start.

I've prayed and prayed
And simple words He gave,
Never telling me the exact day.
Oh, if He had only told me it would be Forever. And. A. Day.

But you are worth the wait.
I knew that from the first day.
God's never late.
His timing just seems to be Forever. And. A. Day.

The promise He gave me,
A simple word about you.
God told me,
"This man will know you so well,
And will love you still."

My heart is so thankful.
You're an answer to many prayers.
So my prayer for you, Mr.
Is that you would know how much I truly care.
I will remain faithful to you.
Praying for you more than most.
I'm your side-kick, Love.
No matter the coast.

I'll go where you go.
I'm with you until the end.

You're my beau.
I promise, I'll write my prayers with a pen.

Forever. And. A. Day.
You have been worth the wait.
I've been praying for you every day.
Praying, one day you will let me hire a maid.

God told me it would be worth it.
Waiting this long.
He told me we'd fit.
And our families would get along.

Answered prayer.
Seriously.
I've been praying forever,
For that specifically.

Today,
Forever. And. A. Day.
Doesn't seem that long.
It's a simple glance, a simple love song.

57. Harvest America 2016

March 8, 2016

Lord, I'm overwhelmed at Your goodness.
There were so many people there.
I simply sat, praying in silence,
As they continued to stream in this year.

I personally lost count.
But, Abba, what I love about You,
You cared about every single person in the crowd.
Each individual soul was of the utmost importance to You.

Only You, Lord, knew every individual heart.
And You had a word for each one.
From the songs, the message, and the graphic art,
You reached the souls needing a touch from the Almighty One.

You speak through Your people,
You speak through art.
You reach every soul,
Right where they are.

You give everyone a gift,
Because it not only impacts the lost,
But encourages the hurting Christian,
Who needs a heavenly touch at no cost.

So many are hurting,
And You care about each one.
I know You were pleased Lord,
With the huge step of faith taken.

You call us to take steps of faith,
Because You are coming back.
Thus, You want us to go big,
Subtly hinting the time we lack.

I know You noticed every little detail,
Every act of sacrifice.
And You were so pleased to tell,
Not only America but the world, the truth of Jesus Christ.

We will go big,
Before we go home.
You've given us a mission:
"Relentlessly chase the lost until they're home."

58. Teach Me

March 13, 2016

Lord, can You teach me how to love.
Because I don't think I know how.
I've tried.
But I've failed somehow.

How do you love,
When you've been bruised?
How do you love,
When you've been betrayed?
Moments when you wonder,
Is love even real,
In this day and age?

And then I see You,
Nailed to the cross.
Bruised and betrayed,
Suffering great loss.

And I see Your love,
Surpassing the cost.
Surrendering all,
To save the lost.

I don't love like that.
Honest heart.
When I'm hurt,
My first response is to depart.

To get away,
From that which caused the pain.
Why stay?
Why remain?

My selfish heart.
Says, "Protect yourself."
Oh, to have Your heart,
That says, "Give of yourself."

Still I wonder,
How do You love?
Please teach me, Lord.
This can only come from above.

To give when hurt,
That's not of this world.
You Jesus gave up everything,
For one pearl.

Will I follow Your example?
And love when hurt.
Will I give up everything,
For one pearl?

59. Seek Him!

Seek Him! Seek Him!
For He is found.
Stand at the foot of the cross,
Stand strong on solid ground.

Onward Christian soldier
The fight is great.
Don't grow weary.
Don't succumb to hate.

Do your duty.
Let your emotions flee.
Take courage.
Begin your day on bended knee.

Seek Him! Seek Him!
For He is found.
Waiting for Your cry,
Waiting to hear your voice's sound.

He hears you.
He does.
And He's given you the strength,
To move and impact the ones He loves.

Hear His voice.
Obey His commands.
Seek to love God and others.
Be bold and take a stand.

60. "Where Is He?"—Mary Magdalene

Where is He?
Where is my King?
What did you do with Him?
Please tell me!

I need Him now.
But He's not here.
He's supposed to be in that tomb.
They made that very clear.

But it's empty.
And He's gone.
Who are you?
You really don't look that strong.

Did you carry Him away?
Tell me!
I will go get Him.
That is MY King!

61. Love's Blessings

March 18, 2016

I'm looking for Your smile.
Your love shining through.
That sweet reminder,
Love's blessings are true.

That Your way may be known on the earth,
Your salvation among all the nations. (**Psalm 67:1-2**)
Lord knowing You are so near,
Eclipses every one of my hesitations.

Let the people praise You, O God;
Let the people praise You, My King.
Oh, let the nations be glad,
Let the nations sing! (**Psalm 67:3-4a**)

Your presence, Your smile,
Brings joy to our heart.
For your love captures us,
You know who we truly are.

Let the people praise You, O God;
Let the people praise You, My King.
Oh, let the nations be glad,
Let the nations sing!

God, our own God, shall bless us,
Shall bless us, He will.
And all the ends of the earth shall fear Him. (**Psalm 67:6-7**)
For His name triumphs over evil.

62. Psalm 68:6

God, You place the lonely in families,
You set prisoners free.
Your presence brings joy.
You plant people like trees.

You bring people together,
Rooted in Christ.
The solitary no longer lonely,
But built up by those who are wise.

A gift from the King,
Guarding His own.
Making sure His children,
Are fit to stand at the foot of heaven's throne.

63. Good to Go!

Shine Your face, Lord! (**Psalm 67:1**)
So I can proclaim Your name.
Wherever You want me,
I will say, "Yes! I'm game!"

The desire to go,
To move in my gift.
I'm searching for my sweetspot.
Does anyone need a lift?

I want to disciple,
I want to listen.
I want to continue to learn and grow,
Knowing You'll give understanding and specific direction.

I hear You say, "Who will go?" (**Isaiah 6:8**)
If I could jump, I would,
But my hops are too low,
So, I'll simply say, "Yes! Pick me. I'm good to go!"

64. Questions for God

Psalm 15

Lord, if I ask You a question,
Will You answer me?
It's a question regarding character,
Worship and integrity.

Who may worship in Your sanctuary?
Who may enter Your presence on Your holy hill?
Is it only those who lead blameless lives,
And do what is right, seeking Your will?

Is it the person who speaks the truth from a sincere heart,
Refusing to slander others,
Or harm their neighbors,
Or speak evil of their friends when asked to describe who they are?

Is it the person who despises persistent sinners,
While honoring the faithful followers of the Lord,
A person who keeps their promises,
Even when those promises hurt?

Is it the person who doesn't charge interest,
On the money they lend?
A person who refuses to accept bribes,
To testify against the innocent?

Will these people stand firm forever,
In the house of the Lord?
Is this the type of worship You want, Lord?
A person with this character and integrity of heart?

65. My Strength

The Lord is my strength,
My Refuge, My Redeemer.
To Him I will call.
To Him I will surrender.

Only to Him.
Only to Him, will I go.
For He is my Everything.
He is my all.

I will pour out my heart.
I will hear His counsel.
His words are so perfect.
I love sitting in His presence, being still.

He is all I need.
Though people fight to take His place.
I will not go to them.
Or even allow them to enter the race.

Jesus is perfect.
He alone revives the soul.
He refreshes, He heals,
He alone makes beautiful things out of all.

66. The Second Vision

Zechariah 1:18-21

Then I raised my eyes and looked,
And saw four horns.
This vision, Lord,
What's it for?

And an angel replied to me,
"These horns represent the world powers,
That scattered the family."

These horns relied on their power and pride,
And went too far.
God did not like it,
So, He's judging them,
And comforting her.

Judah, Israel and Jerusalem were too hurt.
God did not like it,
So, He's sending support.

Then the Lord showed me four craftsmen,
Ready to go.
"What are they doing?
Is this just for show?"

So, He said to me,
"These horns scattered the family,
And oppressed them too much,
So, I'm sending these craftsmen to deal with such."

"The craftsmen will come and terrify the proud,
To cast out the horns that humbled,
And scattered Judah around."

"The craftsmen are strong,
And will throw the proud and powerful down,
The craftsmen will destroy them,
For these people hurt My own."

God loves His people too much,
To let them sit and suffer,
So, He sends someone to deliver,
To relieve the unnecessary terror.

God protects His own,
And won't let them sit oppressed.
He loves His kids,
We can now rest.

67. Opportunity

March 21, 2016

Thank You Lord for giving me,
This gift of life.
So please hold the key,
And open those doors of opportunity,
That You want me,
To run through,
Sharing Christ,
Breaking through,
To every hard heart,

That needs to repent,
And surrender to the One,
Who was heaven sent.

68. Solid Rock

March 21, 2016

On this solid rock I stand,
Arms raised high,
Reaching for His hand.

Surrendering all,
Focused on Christ,
Saying, "Yes" to His call,
Knowing the call comes straight from Jesus Christ.

Moving forward,
While forgetting the past.
Reaching for the prize,
Ready to outlast.

Enduring to the end,
Strengthened by His hand.
Knowing my life will take crazy bends,
As I stand by my man.

69. I Will Surrender

We don't get to choose,
What God allows.
We get to choose,
To surrender and bow.

Hallelujah, Praise the King!
I will surrender,
On bended knee.

To the One who knows.
My life will overflow,
With the presence of my King,
The One who reigns supreme.

To Him I go.
Only Him will I show,
The reverence due.
Only to the King of the Jews.

Hallelujah, Praise the King!
I will surrender,
On bended knee.

70. The Impact of a Life

The impact of a life,
Is more than we know.
God sees.
He knows.

He knows how one word,
Uplifts a heart.
He understands how when one reaches out,
It encourages another right where they are.

He made us to love one another,
So as we support our sister or brother,
We meet those needs,
Often unseen.

It's the call to look beyond our self,
And ask the Lord,
"What's Your will?
Who do You want me to talk to?
Who is in need of prayer or encouragement to be still?"

So often we don't realize,
People remember our words.
They remember that loving touch,
That encouraged them when they were hurt.

It's listening to the voice of the Lord,
And obeying when He calls.
Ministering to the needs,
Of those feeling backed against a wall.

We may never know,
The impact of our life.
But we do know when we reached out to others in the name of Jesus Christ,
He was glorified.

71. Help Me, King

March 30, 2016

Help me King,
To do the right thing.
You've called me to pray and seek,
While waiting on You to speak.

Staying on my knees I wait,
Praying for You to rend my soul,
As I cry out waiting for my anguish to abate,
Trusting You to plead my case.

Trying not to do the wrong thing,
Holding my tongue,
Thanking You for filtering me,
In public when I'm not on my knees.

It's Your grace that holds me steady,
While I face what most aren't ready.
It's You Jesus and Your truth,
That has kept me from coming unglued.

Thank You King for knowing me.
For listening and even correcting me.
It's Your love that draws me back.
Knowing I can just speak my heart without fear or even tact.

And You don't think the wrong thing.
You don't misunderstand.
Or even fear me.
But continue to love me unconditionally.

This type of love overwhelms my soul.
This is the lesson I've learned,
That will never grow old.
Your love is what purifies gold.

72. Seek To Please Him

March 31, 2016

Do you fear the Lord?
Or are you more afraid of man?
Are your actions living the Word?
Or are you living to please them?

Will you stand strong in your convictions,
Knowing they come from God's divine hand?
Or will you succumb to the temptation
Of pleasing men?

God loves you!
And He wants you to seek to please Him.
His purpose for Your life,
Is for you to share the truth of Jesus Christ to all men.

73. A Simple Prayer

March 31, 2016

The difference a simple prayer makes,
Overwhelms my soul.
It is like night and day,
Breaking me free from that stronghold.

Have you ever felt,
So weighed down.
Unable to take a breath,
Feeling bound,
By something unfound,
Yet unmatched by the prayer of one who bows?

I can't explain it.
It's way over my head.
But the darkness has lifted.
And the oppression has left.

My thankful heart,
Rejoices in the Lord.
Praising God for the sincere heart,
Who heard His voice and prayed even more.

Jesus Christ lives.
He defeated death.
And He's alive and moving,
Desiring His heirs to pray and intercede, for the unsaid.

What would the church be like,
If we prayed even more?
Uniting ourselves in humility,
Praying relentlessly for our neighbors?

74. For This Person I Will Pray

April 1, 2016

I don't really understand,
This thing called prayer.
Or even how You want us to be sensitive,
Praying for all Your heirs.

There is a name,
Of someone I've never even met.
So relentless on my heart, Lord,
A constant burden to pray, whenever I see red.

So I pray he casts the net,
That he's not upset,
But seeking You,
Remaining true,
To the Word he knows,
Having the eyes to see what You show.
Putting on the whole armor of God,
Protected by the belt of truth, the helmet of salvation, the breastplate of
righteousness, the shield of faith, the sword of the Spirit and the gospel
shoes he shod.

Moving forward with that vision on his heart,
Understanding You Lord want him to simply do his part.
Using his gifts entirely for Your glory,
Knowing You are writing his life story.
Loving the way it plays out,
Trusting You Lord without a doubt.
Taking those steps of faith,
Crazy steps that call for crazy faith.
Reading Your Word,
Sharing so others learn.

About the love of Jesus Christ.
The Man who died for us, regardless of the price,
Knowing that it pleased You,
To see people come to know Truth.

This man knows he's saved by grace,
Restored to a place,
Of love and devotion,
A life filled, with maybe too much emotion,
But overwhelming love and laughter,
A life full of abundance and character,
Living for Jesus Christ,
Desiring to learn from those that are wise,
Reaching the lost,
No matter the cost,
Wanting more people in heaven,
Thus, sharing the gospel with men and women.

Knowing this life we live,
Is simply a gift.
From the King,
Who reigns over all things.

For this person I will pray,
Seriously not sure why You've burdened my heart,
But I will obey.

Trusting You will hear and answer.
Sometimes I feel like a prayer secret agent,
Coming up under.

Supporting people that I really don't know,
Believing in faith, Lord, this is how You roll.

75. Spiritual Maturity

April 2, 2016

We don't get a choice,
In the trials we face.
But spiritual maturity will reveal,
Whether we handled them well, in this spiritual race.

Training begins in the shadows,
Before the big race.
Some do double days and work hard,
Seeking to set the pace.

The back log of hours,
Spent at God's feet,
Are revealed in the moment,
Keeping one free from defeat.

When the disciples privately asked Jesus,
"Why couldn't we cast it out?"
Jesus' response was simple,
As He explained how.

"This kind can come out by nothing,
But fasting and prayer."
The word to the heart,
You need to spend ample time with the Lord, prior.

You don't know what you will face,
But you know who holds the future.
Best to spend time at Jesus' feet praying,
Trusting He will give You the right words and demeanor.

The Lord wants us to grow,
Responding to difficulties correctly.
He will burden our heart to our weaknesses,
Training us while we're on our knees.

We need more people,
Handling trials and difficult situations well.
So my prayer is that people would hear the Lord's voice,
When He says, "Be still."

76. Rescued

April 4, 2016

For now I see,
With my own eyes I see.
As a shepherd rescues his sheep,
Lord, You rescued me.

As jewels of a crown,
Lifted like a banner over the land. (**Zechariah 9:16**)
Sparkling all around,
For those needing to see God's hand.

You are with me.
You are with me.
I rejoice in that fact alone.
Jesus, Your presence is priceless,
People can't buy what I own.

Lord, You promised You would save me,
And that I would be a blessing to the land. (**Zechariah 8:13**)

I cling to Your promise, Jesus,
Not afraid, but strengthened because of Your hand.

You are with me.
You are with me.
I rejoice in that fact alone.
Jesus, Your presence is priceless,
People can't buy what I own.

77. Fight Until All The Lost Are Won

April 5, 2016

We shall fight because the Lord is with us, (**Zechariah 10:5**)
We shall fight on this battle ground.
Jesus, You are the cornerstone, (**Zechariah 10:4**)
The foundation of this land.

The enemy will not conquer.
For Christ has defeated His foe.
Right now He is choosing to use us,
To beat back the enemies blow.

So though our hands feel weak,
And our hearts are faint,
We press forward,
Rejoicing now with all of the saints.

Jesus is the Victor.
He's defeated death and the grave.
We will fight today to reach the lost,
Knowing Christ wants the lost saved.

One life is so precious,
In the eyes of our Savior, Jesus Christ.
He will leave the 99 to find that one,
No matter the cost, no matter the price.

Jesus Christ is God, (**John 10:30**)
Like the Father, like the Son.
His timing is so perfect, When He says,
"Father, the hour has come." (**John 17:1**)

There is a specific time,
For the will of the Father to be done.
We would be wise to seek the lost now,
Fighting on this battlefield until all of the lost are won. (**2 Peter 3:9**)

78. The Messiah

April 6, 2016

The True Shepherd came,
To seek the lost and save.
He humbled himself and became a man,
Jesus Christ is His name.

Jesus is the Messiah,
Deity in the flesh.
But He was rejected by most,
Even as He breathed His last breath.

His death on the cross saved our lives.
As He forgave us of our sins.
But truly what sets Him apart from the rest,
Is He rose again.

Jesus Christ is alive.
He was raised from the dead to justify. (**Romans 4:25**)
Standing at God's right hand,
He lives today to intercede and pray for all the land, (**Hebrews 7:25**)
Looking forward to when He sees us again.
Waiting for the right time to end all of the sin. (**2 Peter 3:9-10**)

Jesus is coming back.
It will happen in a twinkling of an eye. (**1 Corinthians 15:52**)
We won't have time to pack,
When we hear a shout, a trumpet sound from God, and are caught up in the sky.
(**1 Thessalonians 4:16-17**)

There is a day,
When Jesus Christ will return to the earth.
All the old will pass away.
And perfection will finally be seen and heard.

79. The True Shepherd

The True Shepherd,
Lays down his life for His sheep.
He teaches them how to love.
He teaches them how to weep.

The True Shepherd,
Chases after the lost one.
He leaves the 99,
And rescues His own.

The True Shepherd,
Lives out truth.

He shows His sheep the right way,
To handle disputes.

The True Shepherd,
Cares more for His sheep than Himself,
He doesn't point fingers and cast blame,
He carries their burdens and their shame.

The True Shepherd,
Never falsely accuses.
He knows His sheep so well.
He corrects the wolves whose hurtful words abuse.

The True Shepherd,
Carries a rod and a staff.
A rod to correct;
His staff to comfort, guide and make His sheep laugh.

The True Shepherd,
Set the Ultimate Example,
He laid down His life for His sheep,
Calling us to imitate Him, and follow.

The True Shepherd,
Always sought His Father in heaven,
Who knows what He said in private?
There is a reason.

80. Let All The Redeemed Rejoice!

Let all those rejoice,
Who put their trust in You!

Let them shout for joy,
Because You defend them with truth! (**Psalm 5:11**)

Let those who love Your name,
Rest in joy from above.
For You bless the godly, O Lord,
Surrounding them with Your shield of favor and love. (**Psalm 5:12**)

Rejoice!
All who take refuge in You,
Let them sing joyful praises forever.
Knowing You protect them with truth.

Rejoice!
Rejoice!
Hallelujah!
Rejoice!

You, Lord, have rescued.
Let all the redeemed,
Rejoice!

81. I Love Your Presence

I love Your presence.
When You show up.
Your glory, Lord,
Interrupts.

It interrupts my selfishness.
It opens my eyes to the truth.

Your glory and manifest presence,
Is not just found in a pew.

You are everywhere.
You dwell in the dark cloud, (**1 Kings 8:12**)
Your glory reveals Your approval.
Like a Father, proud.

Would You shine Your face,
On me today?
I want to see You.
As I pray.

82. Your Mercy and Grace, Won

I love You Lord,
And I'm so thankful for all You've done.
Your mercy and grace,
Won.

You defeated the grave,
You forgave,
You saved.
You put others first,
When You Lord, were hurt.
The best example of humility,
Was displayed on the tree,
As You paid,
For my mistake.

In Your love You gave me a choice,
I can still hear Your voice whisper above the noise,

"I've given you this life,
Honor Me and say good-bye,
To everything that is holding you down,
Get rid of that weight that has you bound,
In chains I don't want on you,
Believe me, I want you free, running true.
I'll take care of what you can't control.
Don't worry, I am the One on the throne.
I've given you this passion,
To live out while I'm preparing your mansion,
In heaven, it will be great,
But you still have work to do here today.
So move forward confidently,
Here is the key,
Open this door,
And step into so much more.
Share the gospel with the lost,
Don't be afraid of the cost.
There is an urgency to this mission,
Carry it out, you have My permission.
You don't need any clues,
Because I love you.
Just listen to Me,
And you will succeed."

I truly love You Lord,
And I'm so thankful for all You've done.
Your mercy and grace,
Won.

83. Choose Christ

God's love for the world
Is shown in His Son.
He boldly said, "I have no favorites." **(Romans 2:11)**
And has loved each and every one.

This perfect love,
Has reached so many.
As they have felt accepted,
And adopted into His family.

No jealousy or quarrels,
Found in His family.
Because God loves,
Equally.

His kids have different needs.
And each need He meets.
He can't treat them the same,
Because He has made them all unique.

God's love for His family,
Outmatches the world's superficial love.
Through the death of His Son,
He chose to redeem all of us.

He wants you to be a part of His family,
He will welcome you in.
But you have to choose to surrender,
Repenting of your sin.

Jesus is the only way,
To God the Father.
So, choose Christ,
And live forever.

84. Reborn

May 5, 2016

Even in His own land,
Surrounded by His own.
He was not accepted,
Or even known. (**John 1:10-11**)

But to all who believed in Him,
And accepted Him,
He gave the right to become children of God,
Welcomed in. (**John 1:12**)

They are reborn!
Not a physical birth.
But a rebirth. (**John 1:13**)
Adopted heirs, with Christ—the Word.

The Word became flesh,
And dwelt among man.
Full of unfailing love and faithfulness,
We've seen His glory in this land. (**John 1:14**)

The glory of the only Son of the Father,
Full of grace and truth.
This is Jesus Christ, our Savior.
Who's come to redeem and save the few.

The few who recognize,
And accept Him as their Lord.
Receiving Him into their hearts.
Reborn.

85. Pride

Is your pride,
A weight in another's life?
Holding them back,
From experiencing the freedom found in Christ.

The Son has set you free.
You are free indeed.
So relinquish your control of others,
And live on bended knee.

This life is not about you.
Stop the selfishness.
Repent and ask for forgiveness,
Seeking their best instead.

When are we more like Christ?
When we give up our life,
Forgive and pray,
Letting go of our pride.

You are not your brother's keeper.
They submit to God,
Not you.
So let go, and focus on the truth.

Where are your thoughts?
Are they on Jesus Christ?
Or are you so focused on this other person,
Missing what's truly important in this life.

Focus on Jesus.
Keep your eyes on Him.
This life will bring crazy bends.
But your race was designed by Him.

Stop looking at their race.
Don't even think about trying to control it.
Your pride will be,
The roadblocks that will defeat it.

As a Christian, you are not called to control.
You are called to submit to God,
Who is the only One,
Worthy to oversee and hold the rod.

Throw off every weight and sin, (**Hebrews 12:1**)
That so easily ensnares you.
Could that very weight and sin,
Be the pride that is controlling you?

Humble yourself under the mighty hand of God.
Recognizing that it is the humility of Christ,
That taught,
Us how to put others first in this life.

Humility forgives others,
And asks for forgiveness.
Why?
Because in both cases, it's others focused.

This life is not about you.
You are here to glorify God, doing His will.
He loves you though,
But recognize Jesus experienced more than you ever will.

So instead of trying to control other Christians,
Focus on your own race instead.
How about coming up under and supporting them,
Instead of tearing them down like worldly women and men.

There is a huge cloud of witnesses,
Watching you race.
Maybe your eyes should be focused on Jesus,
So you will be the one setting the pace.

I'm just on the outside,
Looking in.
This is what I see,
Don't hate, just forgive.

86. For all the Dads

May 6, 2016

Sometimes you just need a little guidance.
A quick word from the wise.
"Dad! How do I get home?"
And obeying without asking why.

You know who to call.
The moment crisis arises.
The one who always picks up the phone.
The faithful, the wise.

Dads have a special gift,
Given from the Lord.

It's the unconditional love in their heart for their kids,
Reflecting their Savior.

The godly men set the example,
As they lead their family,
Instilling great truths,
Saying, "Follow me."

The legacy they leave,
Impacts more than they know.
It's the legacy of one,
Who knows the Lord and makes Him known.

When a prayer needs to be said,
For any event,
Dad is normally the one asked,
Because his sincere faith ministers to the hearts of the men and women.

Dad's giving heart,
Doesn't stop when their kids are young.
They keep giving and meeting the needs,
Of their children who are grown.

Nothing quite matches,
Dad's love and kindness.
You know it's genuine,
When he's still there when your life seems to be a mess.

"This is what my Dad did,"
I heard so often.
I love the godly legacy left in my family,
As the men followed the example of the older men.

What is a great legacy,
That will impact your family?

It's when the men love God with their heart, soul, and mind, and their neighbors as themselves,
And say, "Follow me."

Not a perfect life,
But a life seeking the Lord.
A life reaching out to others in Jesus' name,
So much so that others are reborn.

What a gift,
To be able to watch Dad,
Reaching out to others with the love of Christ,
Right where God has placed him in this land.

I love you Dad,
And am so thankful for your godly example.
I love the legacy you are leaving,
As you have made sure our joy buckets are full,
And we are prepared for eternity.

87. Love Their Example

May 6, 2016

What is true love?
I'm not sure I know.
But I do love watching others,
Who seem to just glow.

It doesn't matter their age.
In fact, the most beautiful,
Are the elderly as they engage,

Talking with each other,
Loving eyes full, not recognizing they are center stage.

My favorite example,
I witnessed at work.
I just knew the Lord wanted me to see this.
The love of a husband, elevating his wife's true worth.

When Ivan and Joyce first walked in,
One glance and you knew the love they had for each other,
Exceeded worldly exterior and resonated deep within.

In their 80's, as beautiful as ever.
They walked in holding hands,
You knew they meant forever,
When they entrusted their lives into each other's hands.

Joyce had dementia.
Ivan was a POW in WWII,
Their story is amazing.
I sat listening to them with a pen and didn't move.

"Where's my husband?"
Joyce would always ask.
She didn't speak much,
This was one of the few clear sentences I ever heard her ask.

"Joyce! Ivan's right here."
She would turn her head and see him,
Her panic immediately cleared,
As she rested her eyes on her husband.

I was so curious about their marriage,
So being nosey I asked,
"Ivan! What's the secret to your marriage?"
He answered with two words, "Jesus Christ."

They had been married for over 60 years.
I loved the testimony of how they came to Christ.
They did not grow up believers,
In fact, they despised those Christians, thinking them unwise.

But then Joyce went to a women's Bible study,
When Ivan was stationed in Washington DC.
She accepted the Lord,
And was afraid of what her husband would think.

She came home from the study.
And stood at the door.
She said, 'Ivan I'm changed."
And he internally said, "Ok I'm going to test this, to see more."

He purposefully did things to provoke her.
She used to get so angry.
And amazingly enough, he said,
She was as kind as could be.

"There is something to this,"
He thought to himself.
Then he started researching the Word,
And came to the decision, Jesus Christ is alive and well.

He accepted Jesus Christ as his Lord and Savior,
And their marriage changed forever.
When you look at the love they have for each other,
You would never know, they hadn't known the Lord for forever.

Curious, I asked Joyce the same question.
"Joyce, what's the secret to your marriage?"
I will never forget her immediate simple response even with dementia,
"He's nice to me," was all she cared.

Her response changed my outlook on the attitudes of men.
How simply being nice to a woman,
Is what impacts her when she can't think clearly, in the end.

Joyce didn't speak much.
But I would ask her the same questions all the time.
Her answers were always, "He's nice to me,"
And "Where is my husband?"

Joyce glowed even in her advanced age.
She didn't have to speak,
Her smile shined the light of Jesus Christ,
For all to see.

I loved that they always held hands.
And I would think,
"That's the marriage I want,
When I'm older and can't even think."

It's that confident trust,
Born over time.
A love unexplainable,
A best friend for all time.

There was a day,
And this impacted me again.
People should never discount,
Their example to those watching.
We had to teach Joyce fall recovery.
Because when she fell, she didn't know how to get back up.
The struggle for Ivan,
In his advanced age, he couldn't pick her up and help.

We had to get Joyce sitting on the ground.
In her dementia state, this scared her,
Because she didn't understand.

The most beautiful thing I saw,
The true love of a husband.
80+ year old Ivan,
Got himself down on the ground,
To sit next to his wife,
In order to comfort her,
And guide her.

We scared her.
But she was fine with him.
The whole trust thing was witnessed,
As she didn't listen to us, but to him.

If you could just picture,
Two 80+ year olds sitting on the ground,
Their feet out in front of them,
While they are holding hands.

The minute Ivan got down on the ground,
Joyce grabbed for his hand,
And clung to her man.

"Joyce, this is how you do this,"
Ivan said in a sweet voice.
As 80+ year old Ivan,
Demonstrated the fall recovery with poise.

With tears in my eyes,
I watched his love for his wife.
Teaching her how to,
Recover from falls with dignity and pride.

I will never forget,
What Joyce told to me.
So I wrote in my bible,
"I want my husband to be nice to me."

When we can't think clearly,
It's the simple things we will remember.
How love is truly displayed,
When we are kind to one another.

I absolutely love their example,
It's one of the best I've witnessed.
I will remember it forever,
Thanking Jesus.

88. Thankful For My Parents

May 7, 2016

I am so thankful for my parents.
The Lord blessed me with them.
Never controlling,
Just guiding, pointing to Him.

Jesus Christ, my Lord and Savior,
Instilled in me young,
As I learned from my Father and Mother,
Who taught all us kids and made the Bible fun.

I cringe when I'm around those who seek control,
I am so not used to it,
Because my parents instilled in us the value of trust,
And the beauty and treasure that comes with it.

I am so thankful for the example they set,
Telling us kids to seek God and pray,

Giving us their advice,
But never controlling our every move like some do today.

My mom is a giver.
She seems to know what we all need.
I don't even have to say it.
She just shows up and brings the exact thing,
That I need.

My dad is actually the poet,
Not me.
I might have got it from him,
I know he is so proud of me.

He wrote me a poem
For my birthday a few years ago.
A treasure for sure,
I've kept it secure.

It started by saying:
"Happy Birthday Alysa

Today is a special day where we celebrate you,
Your birthday is today, be blessed in all you do.

We remember very well the Sunday you were born,
We headed to the hospital at 3:00 am that morn.

You made your arrival six and a half hours later,
I was there helping your mother breathe much greater.

You were beautiful then as you are right now,
And I went off to church to take a little bow.

I went in the back door as they started to sing,
Phil Northcut stopped right then as he saw me come in.

'A baby girl is born today,' I announced to the room.
Dixie and baby are "A" Ok and everyone cheered with a boom.

Then everyone sang (My Tribute) 'To God be the glory for the things He
has done,'
He gave us you Alysa and we knew everything would be fun.

You started out with dance and you always did well in school.
Later came soccer, then college, where you rowed with Crew.

You have a love for God and to us that is number one.
Thank you for growing into the woman you've become.

We want you to know that we will love you forever.
Happy Birthday to you Alysa, may God guide your every endeavor."

Thank you Lord for my parents,
A gift from You, King,
As my dad always says,
"We are blessed to be a blessing."

89. The Passion On My Heart

May 7, 2016

The passion on my heart,
The burden of my soul,
Is to see others meet Jesus,
Before they grow old. (**Ecclesiastes 12:1-8**)

To know God
And to make Him known.

Here and now,
While they are still young.

Who knows what will happen,
In the days to come.
God is the One who knows the number,
He knows when Jesus will return or when He will call us home.

There is no time to waste.
Now is the time.
Don't spend your time uselessly.
But redeem the time.

Tell others about Jesus.
Plant that seed.
Look for the opportunity,
To pray for all those who are in need.

The passion on my heart,
The burden of my soul.
Is to write the words God shares with me,
Before I grow old.

To know God,
And to make Him known.
With the gift He has given me,
Before Jesus returns or He calls me home.

It's not like I'm sick.
I'm as healthy as can be.
The thing is, we truly do not know the day Jesus will return,
Or when God will call us home, for He holds the key.

What's the passion on your heart?
What's the burden of your soul?

Are you ready to impact all those around you,
Before Jesus returns or God calls you home?

Now is the time
To redeem the time.
To pray and ask the Lord,
For the open door.

90. My Prayer For Your Bride

May 13, 2016

My prayer for Your Bride,
Is that she would have a flame of affection,
In her heart, soul and mind.

Loving You with every ounce,
Of her being.
Rejoicing!

Singing!
Dancing!
Writing!
Creating!

Looking to You in awe.
Living solely,
For the glory of God. (**1 Corinthians 10:31**)

91. Godly Love

We want to be loved,
We want grace,
We love it when God showers us with blessings,
Even when we have dirt on our face.

But will we love others,
When we see their true self?
When we see their character flaws and sinful nature,
That's often hidden from those who don't know them well?

Will we give grace,
To those who have hurt us dearly?
Knowing they, too, are simply human,
And have moments of failure not always living for God's glory.

So often we go through life,
Wanting to be known and yet loved,
But we fail to reciprocate,
And show godly love.

You know me,
And you love me.
Thank you for loving me,
Even when I'm stubborn, not seeing clearly.

I know you,
And I love you.
In a godly way,
As a sister in the Lord,
Simply desiring you to be walking in holiness today.

92. "It Girl"

Clean hands and a pure heart,
Will set you apart.
In today's world,
As culture is constantly looking for the new "It Girl."

There will always be a new girl.
Face it.
That should not be your goal, girl,
Get with it.

Seek to please an audience of One,
For your true reward is in heaven,
Where you've already won.

You are accepted.
You are loved.
And you don't have to do anything,
To earn that love.
Regardless of what you do,
Your Father in heaven is proud of you.

He loves you.
He knows you.
He knows everything they said about you,
That is not true.
He knows what is happening right now,
Which to you seemed to come out of the blue.
He loves you.
And that will never change.
In His eyes you will remain,
Forever His little girl,
Formed to, yes, impact this world.

Jesus' death and resurrection,
Saved you from the world's rejection.
As you stay focused on Christ,
You will walk through this life,
Driven to succeed,
Ready to lead,
In what He is calling you to do,
Not what the world thinks you should do.

The world may like you today,
And hate you tomorrow.
Face it.
That's life, but don't quit.

Remember when You seek to please an audience of One,
Everyone else becomes blurry,
And you've already won,
Because you are living for God's glory,
Allowing Him to write your life story,
Not worried about those in the world,
Who will like you today,
But hate you tomorrow when they meet the new "It Girl."

Clean hands and a pure heart,
Will set you apart.
It's God's will for your life.
Walking like Christ,
Seeking to please an audience of One,
Knowing, in His eyes, you've already won,
Because you did exactly what He told you to do.
You prayed, you read His Word and you shared God's worldview,
With all those needing a biblical cue,
As to what to do,

With their life,
So when they meet Christ,
They will know they made the best decision,
And now their life has taken on a new meaning and direction,
Because you simply obeyed Christ,
Not all the confusing voices vying for authority in your life.

You have fought the good fight,
And when you finish your race,
God will say, "Well done good and faithful servant,"
He might even include, "You did awesome at setting the pace."

93. When God says, "Pray"

May 23, 2016

When God says, "Pray."
We pray.
For God is the One,
That motivates us to pray.
And if He is prompting us to pray,
We better obey.

94. Jesus' Example

When your heart is full of pride,
And hardened from life's trials.
Remember your Savior, Jesus Christ,
Who wore wounds well.

He lived a perfect life,
But was mocked and scorned.
He was rejected by most,
And yet, it was us for whom He mourned.

He had perfect communion,
With God the Father.
He had something we didn't,
But longed for our walk to go further.

Look at how He handled,
The cost of life's trials.
Yes, He bore scars,
But He wore them well.

He wanted us to experience,
What He had.
So He died a cruel and torturous death,
And rose again.

Jesus' example,
Is one for the books.
He handled life's trials the best.
Something we should not overlook.

He knows what we are going through,
For He experienced it Himself.
What you are facing today is not new,
Look to Him and His example for help.

95. Calm Amidst Chaos

June 7, 2016

This calm amidst chaos,
Is not of the world.
It's You, Jesus,
Your peace unfurled.

Peace.
The absence of fear.
The calm on a heart.
Knowing Jesus is near.

Fear.
Allows chaos to reign.
Worry so gripping,
The heart constrained.

How in the world,
Do we obtain this peace?
So, our heart doesn't constrict,
But remains firm, planted like a tree.

Jesus, You're the only way.
Would we see that so clear?
Your perfect love amidst the chaos,
Calms our heart and takes away all fear.

Your love meets our very need.
You know us so well.
Would we surrender to You today,
Would we seek You and be still?

You died on the cross,
So we wouldn't live in torment.
Would we recognize that,
And live our life without it.

Fear torments a heart,
Taking away all joy.
Leaving one missing out,
On the abundant life, full of beautiful noise.

Your death made a way,
For us to live without fear.
You died on the cross,
So that we could draw near.

My prayer today,
Is that we would remember,
We can have calm amidst the chaos,
Because we stand in Your presence forever.

96. Step into History

June 12, 2016

Some people have different experiences.
All allowed by God.
Ultimately, God protects all of His children.
Nothing happens without His approval or nod.

God's plan for you,
God's plan for me,

Is a story He will unfold,
As we step into history.

Jesus simply calls us to abide,
To trust Him,
And not hide,
But to walk worthy as His Bride.

Are we ever truly ready,
For what comes our way?
Maybe our step remains steady,
Maybe it has a little sway.

What do you do when the experience isn't the best?
Do you hold onto your grudge,
Do you withhold forgiveness?
Or pray and let it rest?

Do you keep bringing it back up,
That's a temptation, for sure.
Or do you forgive and let up?
Wanting the same in return.

Best to not hold a grudge,
But to seek the Lord.
Pray when you get the nudge.
Pray even more.

Forgiveness is a daily thing.
You want it too.
You fail all of the time,
Yet expect grace and the truth.

Don't compare your experience,
To all the others,

That might only bring despair,
Just remember, God loves you and covers.

To the one who experienced something amazing,
Rejoice now,
And take hold of that wing,
Keep soaring,
Rejoicing,
Proclaiming,
Surrendering,
Keep moving forward,
For the King.

Those sweet moments of joy,
His presence so near,
Makes my breath catch,
Makes my eyes tear.

Lord when You show up,
I love it so much.
I'm a little addicted to Your entrance,
Your glory,
Your love.

You just have this way,
Of making Your presence known.
I know I experienced it today,
As You loved on Your own.

So much going on,
In the world today.
Chaos still reigns
But the Holy Spirit holds it at bay.

Though, there will be a day,
When You take Your own home.

That moment is coming,
When God will say,
"Son, it's time. Go rescue Your Bride. Bring her home."

The experiences we face today,
Whether we think they are good or bad,
Can we for a moment change our perspective,
And see Your presence so near in the fire we called "bad."

I don't necessarily want to go through some things again,
If I had a choice.
But Lord, I know You were with me.
You carried me through with Your voice.

You are the Best Communicator ever.
Can I just say that?
You talk to me all off the time,
And that is what held my heart intact.

Now if we could only have,
More of those mountaintop experiences here on earth.
But wait, we can!
Every time we pray and read God's Word.

So those experiences we face,
Whether good or bad,
Lord Jesus we thank You,
For being the Sovereign Lord over all the land.

Everything we have faced,
Passed first through the loving hands of our Father.
Yes, He allowed these experiences in your life.
And as you walked through fire, He drew closer.

It's always good to remember that those very experiences,
Those steps of history,

Simply prepare our heart,
For the Grand Entrance of our King.

97. God Chose You

July 7, 2016

God chose you specifically, (**Acts 9:15**)
Because He loves you.
He knows you.
He's pleased with you.

Nothing you do today,
Will make Him love you more.
All He wants from you is that you'd stay,
In His presence, thankful for all of the open doors. (**Matthew 11:28-30**)

All of your accomplishments,
Are gifts from Him.
Heaven sent,
So that you can glorify Him. (**1 Corinthians 10:31**)

Even those moments, (**John 21:3-17**)
When you feel like your life is such a waste,
Failure rings in your head,
Just wait.

Wait on Him, (**Psalm 27:14**)
And seek His face. (**Jeremiah 29:13**)
And remember even if your heart condemns you, (**1 John 3:20**)
God is greater and He designed your race.

What you see as failure,
To Him may be success.
The world doesn't have His eyes, (**Revelation 1:14**)
And His eyes see above all the rest.

God loves you, (**John 3:16**)
And that will never change.
He is the One constant you have in life. (**Malachi 3:6**)
Don't worry, He will never change.

He is the Alpha, the Omega, (**Revelation 1:11**)
The Beginning and End.
He is Sovereign over all the world,
And your life is in His hands. (**John 10:29**)

98. *Finish Strong!*

July 7, 2016

Finish strong!
Finish strong!
This race you are in,
Finish strong!

You may be weary,
Wanting this season to end.
But just know this, my friend,
God will see you through until the end.

Seasons come,
And seasons go.

You can't get seasons back,
So keep throwing those seeds and sow.

Sow a great harvest,
Right where you are,
When the Lord wants you to move,
He'll open the door.

My friend—
Your work for the Lord is not in vain,
So be steadfast, immoveable,
Abounding right where you are and you will gain. (**1 Corinthians 15:58**)

A rich insight into the Lord,
His grace and so much more,
His whisper to your heart,
Explaining why you are still where you are.

You really won't know,
How many people you impacted for the Lord.
Best to not know now,
Just stay on your knees and bow.

For there will be a day,
When you meet those souls in heaven,
And see all those lives saved,
And you will understand why your life had a prolonged season.

Make the most of this season,
For change will come.
Finish strong, friend.
Finish strong.

99. Safe Haven

July 18, 2016

The world is dark.
It seems to only be getting worse.
Lord! The enemy's hits have left a mark,
Many are crumbling, needing to seek You first.

We need You,
As we face this overwhelming turmoil.
We need a safe haven,
In this world.

Lord Jesus, You provide, You deliver.
You knew our every need when You came.
You died on the cross covering us in ultimate conquer,
With blood, backed by the power of Your name.

You are safe, You are secure,
You know everything already.
You are our safe haven,
Our rock of refuge, standing firm, ready.

Ready to welcome,
Everyone hurt in this world.
There is so much going on Lord,
They need to know You care about their world.

The experiences everyone faces,
Are similar, yet different.
They need to know You care about every one of them,
And You see their needs as they feel swept away in a current.

"Where are You, Lord?"
So many cry out.
Lord, You are in the church.
Would they see that and not doubt?

My prayer today, is that we Your church,
Would step it up.
And leave a mark on the world,
So, they know what's up.

Jesus Christ saves.
He is alive and ready.
He is present in His church,
Everyone is welcome, it's free.

You knew we would need,
A place that is safe.
You, Jesus, built Your church,
Knowing the world would continue to hate.

When You say it's safe?
What do You mean?
What's the definition of safe,
In a world that justifies "mean."

Safe means one is free from danger,
Damage or harm.
They are secure having escaped injury,
Protected in a trusted atmosphere that will sound an alarm.

You see everyone as valuable,
No one is considered better than the other.
Your church is a safe haven,
For everyone willing to come up under.

You, and Your name.
Jesus Christ, the Son of the Father.
The One who will never change,
Immanuel, the Prince of Peace, our Provider.

Jesus, You are coming back.
The world will only get worse.
Until the day You return,
Would the people know our safe haven is found in the church?

100. Prepare to Meet God

August 2, 2016

Are you ready to meet God?
See Him face to face?
Hear His voice speak to you,
As He goes over how you ran your race?

Prepare to meet God. (**Amos 4:12**)
Prepare today.
You never know when He will call you home.
Or when Jesus will return, it could be any day.

Redeem the time.
It is essential.
God placed you right where you are for a reason.
He didn't just say, "Oh, she's got potential."

No! He said, "You're it!
I placed you there because you fit!

You are the best person,
To do the job and get it done."

"Reach out to those lost,
And share the message of Christ,
No matter the cost.
Believe me it's worth the price."

What should we do,
To prepare to meet God?
How about we just ask where we will glorify Him best,
And do that job?

It doesn't matter where,
We use our gifts.
As long as we are in His will,
There we will fit.

Now is the time,
To seek the Lord even more.
Can you hear Him calling out,
"Who will go for me? I've opened a door."

There are so many opportunities everyday,
To glorify God,
If we'd only say,
"Here I am! I'll go" or "Ok! I'll stay!"

Sometimes the biggest moments in life,
Are actually found in what some deemed small.
That kind act when you gave a hug to someone who was hurting,
Walking down the hall.

You never know how God will use you,
In the life of someone else,

And how that small act,
Will impact and encourage others as well.

What's the point of this life,
If we can't glorify God with every act,
Or ask Him to bless our decisions that create strife,
As we tell people it's ok to go behind others' backs.

That's not godly.
It only creates division.
People will forgive,
But they will never trust those who made that decision.

When we prepare to meet God,
We need to watch how we use our time.
Are our actions and decisions giving people the wrong mindset,
Encouraging them to sin in ways that will hurt other people's minds.

What will God say,
If that is our last act on earth?
Will he be pleased?
Or will He only see all those who were unnecessarily hurt?

Redeem the time,
Reach out to the lost,
Encourage the hurting,
Use your gifts, no matter the cost.

Recognize how your life does affect others.
Your decisions can hurt,
Or encourage your sisters and brothers.

This life is not about you.
It's about giving God the glory.
Will You ask Him today, "How can I best glorify you?
Please I want people to only see You in my life story."

Prepare to meet God.
Redeem the time.
Glorify God.
And He will renew your mind.

101. I Hear Your Voice Say, "Forgive."

Lord, You are with me,
Whispering to my heart.
I hear Your voice say, "Forgive,"
I hear it brushing across my heart.

They had no clue,
The damage done.
But You Lord forgave them,
Just like You've forgiven me because of Your Son.

You sent Your only Son,
To die the death I deserved.
You forgive everyone,
Who repents and turns from the evil in this world.

I can picture my 4-year-old niece even now,
Holding up that prickly toy crown,
As I looked down at Your Word,
She said, "This is the crown of hurts."

Exactly!
It's the crown of hurts.
Pressed into Your head
Piercing for all it was worth.

Imagining Your pain,
Makes my heart freeze.
Thank You Lord Jesus,
For dying for me.

Lord, You have been with me every step.
I knew You were so near.
Especially that one night I was driving and crying,
And I saw the license plate that said, "IM HERE!"

Lord, You are with me
Whispering to my heart.
I hear Your voice say, "Forgive,"
I hear it brushing across my heart.

I forgive,
Jesus I do.
I forgive those who misunderstood,
And caused issues that pierced me through and through.

It is a new day,
You've renewed my mind.
I will never forget,
But so ever thankful You saved me, right on time.

Those moments You showed up,
Assuring my heart,
Are moments I will never forget,
As You stepped in to heal what they tore apart.

Lord, You are with me,
Whispering to my heart.
I hear Your voice say, "Forgive,"
I hear it brushing across my heart.

102. Seasons

There is a time for everything,
A season for everything under the sun. (**Ecclesiastes 3:1**)
A time to sit.
A time to run.

Every day we are given,
From our Lord Jesus Christ,
No matter the color of the sky,
Is a gift called life.

Our emotions may change,
From day to day.
But while we laugh or cry,
Jesus prays (**Hebrews 7:25**).

People will change.
Circumstances too.
However, Jesus stays the same, (**Hebrews 13:8**)
He's the One constant—the glue.

He is the One constant you have in life,
And that is what makes life awesome.
No matter what you face,
He's there; sometimes He's the only One.

Jesus will never change. (**Malachi 3:6**)
He's given that promise to you.
He is so ever present in your life,
He literally has the best view.

And the sweet part is,
He holds your hand through all the changes,

So, you transition gracefully in this land.
Ready for all the different stages.

103. Accepted, Adopted, Adorned

August 5, 2016

What does it mean to be accepted?
Adopted?
Adorned?

Is there any hope in this life,
For community to come together,
Under one banner—
Jesus Christ, our Lord?

A Christian community of people,
Moving in the same direction,
Is important in today's world,
Which needs to see Redemption.

Jesus Christ came,
To seek and to save.
He died on the cross,
For us to be renamed.

The Ultimate Man,
He showed us how to live,
He showed us how to pray,
He showed us how to give.

What do we see in community today?
Do we see people imitating Christ,
Reaching out to the lost and hurting,
Praying and giving, shining the light?

Because of Christ's death on the cross,
We are accepted in the Beloved.
Our sin, our flaws separated us from God,
But Jesus, the Ultimate Man, took the hit for His Beloved.

Not caring whether His image would be marred.
Yes, He lived a perfect life,
But He was constantly accused, wounded and scarred,
So His Beloved could experience eternal life.

That's the love of our God,
Accepting us.
Sending His Son to take the hit,
That was meant for us.

We are accepted into the family.
Outsiders no more.
God loves us that much.
He turned the barrier into a door.

God adopted us. (**Ephesians 1:5**)
God the Father!
He chose us,
Simply because He loves us.

He made it official,
When He sent His Son,
To earth on a mission,
To redeem all His chosen ones.

Chosen.

Whose chosen?

Are some left out?

No! God has no favorites, (**Romans 2:11**),

He loves the world beyond a shadow of a doubt. (**John 3:16**)

But not everyone in the world loves Him, it's a fact.

And in His love for us,

He lets us choose whether we want to love Him back.

It's your choice,

As to whether you want to accept Him.

He wants to adopt you,

But you have to let Him in.

Do you see your sin?

Your need for a Savior?

God the Father saw your need,

So He sent you a Redeemer.

But you have to repent of your sin, (**Acts 3:19**)

And accept Jesus Christ into your life. (**Romans 10:9**)

He loves you.

Will you receive His love tonight?

If you accept Jesus Christ into your heart,

You are forgiven. (**Romans 10:9**)

God loves you so much He's adorned you with Christ, (**Colossians 3:12**)

You're covered; you're a new creation. (**2 Corinthians 5:17**)

He covered you with the perfect image of His Son.

Jesus Christ is your Beloved,

His image is now yours to own.

You're accepted.

You're adopted.

You're adorned.
You are saved.

You don't have to fear tomorrow,
Because Your Beloved will be with you,
Holding your hand,
As you reach out to those who need Him too.

The world needs to see Redemption,
God redeeming mankind from their sin,
Through His most loving decision,
The death of His loved Son for all of creation.

Does your community display this love?
Accepting?
Adopting?
Adorning?
The outcasts who need to experience God's redeeming love?

It's my prayer today,
That every Christian Community,
Would wake up and see,
God's redeeming love has to be witnessed in you and me,
By the world needing to see the man nailed on the tree,
Redeeming and rescuing for heaven's eternity.

We are accepted.
Adopted.
Adorned.
God the Father loved us that much, (**John 3:16**)
He sent His Son to die for the world.

Will you love Him back today?
And say yes and pray,
Accepting Christ into your heart,
Living in perfect fellowship with the One who knows and loves your heart.

Will your community imitate God's love today? (**Ephesians 5:1**)
As adopted heirs will they reach out and pray,
Wanting others to experience God's eternal love,
By accepting, adopting, adorning those with the gift of love,
The perfect gift that comes straight from above. (**James 1:17**)

104. Hannah

1 Samuel 1
August 6, 2016

Just a little word to those listening,
Never good to have two wives.
Seriously, dude, what were you thinking?
That's like someone trying to catch falling knives.

This happens in more ways than one.
The jealous wife seeing her husband,
Lust after another woman.

But imagine him actually loving another,
Another wife,
One who could actually make him a father?

While you stayed barren,
Longing for children,
Experiencing this other woman constantly glaring,
At you while you sit, wishing you were around the men.

Jealousy shows itself in different forms.
Poor Hannah already struggling,
Not experiencing her dream or the open door,

While this other woman shoves her gifts in Hannah's face, hurting,
Hannah even more.

Hannah could not bear her husband children,
While this other woman could.
This woman had what Hannah wanted,
But it wasn't enough until she was understood.

Women fight for attention.
The jealousy can get ugly.
Those who have what others desire, shun,
Those hurting, making themselves unlovely.

People always seem to want more,
When God has given them so much.
Why do they hurt others by closing the door?
Making it clear that they obviously don't have the right touch.

This other woman provoked Hannah severely,
So badly Hannah was miserable.
Every time they went to the House of the Lord,
The provoking continued until it became unbearable.

Yearly they would go worship and sacrifice to the Lord,
Elkanah, the husband, would make offerings,
For his other wife and all her children in one accord.
But to Hannah he gave a double portion, for he loved her even more.

But Hannah remained miserable,
She just wanted her dream to come true.
While this other woman who had what she wanted,
Kept provoking her until she came unglued.

One day, weeping so badly,
Hannah could not eat.

Her husband tried to console her,
"Babe, can you please eat some meat?"

"Hannah why do you weep,
Why do you not eat?
Why is your heart grieved?
Don't you love me?
Aren't I better than 10 sons?"
Men, don't ever say that to your woman.

It is hard when you heart longs for something great,
But God calls you to wait.
You pray and you pray.
And yet for you, God continues to say, "Wait."
You see doors open for other people,
You wonder why they don't open for you.
You want to rejoice for those and their happy soul,
While you weep in your heart, longing for an open door too.

Some people,
But not all.
Do provoke people,
Enough to the point they might fall.

Mean spirited,
Full of jealousy.
They keep the doors closed,
When they already have what one is praying for, on bended knee.

No, I'm not talking about you.
Unless your heart is convicted,
And you did keep a door closed, too,
Due to your jealousy, keeping others restricted.

Do you think Hannah and this other woman,
Could have been friends?

Couldn't this other woman have recognized Hannah's heart,
And prayed for her instead?

But by provoking and pointing out what Hannah didn't have,
Making Hannah suffer even more;
She herself closed the door,
On a friendship which could have blessed her even more.

Hannah went to the house of the Lord to pray,
Pouring her heart out to God, this day,
Wouldn't you know she was misunderstood by the priest,
Seriously, can't a girl talk to God without someone thinking the least.

He thought she was drunk.
He thought she was crazy.
Come on dude!
Get your heart in line with the Man upstairs, today.

God heard Hannah's selfless prayer,
As she sweetly prayed for the Lord to look upon her affliction,
And remove the affliction,
Remembering her,
With a male heir.

"I'll give him back to You," Hannah prayed.
"He's Yours, Lord,
From the very first day."

God blessed Hannah with a son.
He did.
Samuel was born to this woman.
The prophet was her kid.

Sometimes in life,
We go through crazy seasons.

Heartache and trial happens when there is more than one wife.
Men don't do this, there is no reason.

It's a matter of the heart,
For some.
Repentance is needed in every heart,
Not just one.

For Hannah it was a matter of trust.
God had an amazing plan for her,
Her child would leave most in his dust.
Chasing after God, flying high like a bird.
He would reach many a heart
Speaking God's heart—the Word.

God has a time for everything,
A season for everything under the sun.
If He's called you to wait like Hannah,
He may just want to bless you with a prophet, a son.

Or a girl.
Girls are pretty awesome, too.
All I'm saying is,
God has eternity in view.

105. God's Hand Guiding

August 8, 2016

Those moments when you look back,
And see,
God's hand guiding you with tact,
Through all of the crazy.

You're thankful.
Thankful God cares.
The love of God surpasses,
Any worry, trial, or glare.

Nothing compares,
His Presence has been so clear,
His hand guiding and steady,
Guarding you from all of your fears.

I'm so thankful,
That guarding presence,
Protecting me from those,
Who don't care about life's essence.

A gift,
From God.
A precious gift,
Seriously there's so much power in a simple nod.

Not everyone would get it,
Maybe a few,
Those who know are thankful,
For the guarding presence in the pew.

God moves through people,
He sets them apart,
The gift of a guarding presence,
Protects a heart.

106. God is Able

August 8, 2016

God, You are able to do exceedingly, abundantly,
More than I could ever think or ask. (**Ephesians 3:20**)
Nothing is too hard for You,
Not even this task.

You are able to deliver me from this fire, (**Daniel 3**)
Not sure why I'm in here—who listened to the liar?
But You are able, I know.
Jesus Your presence in this fire with me, is not just for show.

You are able to provide for all of my needs, (**Philippians 4:19**)
I'm so thankful.
I've seen You show up powerfully to feed,
Me when I was hungry, until I was full.

You are able to make me strong, (**Romans 16:25**)
I have nothing to fear.
I want to shout out the message of Jesus Christ,
For all to hear.

You are able to save those who come to You, (**Hebrews 7:25**)
It's just what you do.
You pray and intercede,
And overcome all of the dudes.

You are able to strengthen me when I'm tempted, (**Hebrews 2:18**)
For you were tempted like me.
You know exactly what I need.
That's why You've given Your Word, so I'm planted like a tree. (**Psalm 1:3**)

You are able to perform Your promises, (**Romans 4:20**)
Those precious promises You keep.
Those promises are backed by the power of Your name,
Jehovah—the covenant keeping God, is Your identity.

107. Can't Sleep

August 8, 2016

Sometimes I wonder why I can't sleep.
Lord, do You want me to pray or read?
Do You want me to drink Sleepy Time tea?

Moments when I think,
There's someone who needs prayer.
Sometimes I don't know who though,
So, I listen with a sensitive ear.

Or maybe You have placed a word on my heart.
You want me to write it down now,
So I'll remember it, just like art.
The moment is key,
I don't want to miss the opportunity,
Like any creative person knows,
What's here today,
May be gone tomorrow, that's just how it goes.
Some don't get it.
They think this just happens.
Because you show up with work,
They don't see the hard work that takes place before you even pick up a pen.

But You Lord know,
You've given everyone different gifts.
Some people don't understand,
It's ok, they've got their own gift.

108. Abba, My Heart

August 13, 2016

Abba, my heart.
Moments when I don't like it.
I know You see it,
Moments when I wish I could hide it.

How are we supposed to handle,
The issues we face?
The constant issues,
That don't seem to change?

I've waited and prayed.
Prayed some more and waited.
Moments when I wonder,
How much longer?

But what I love about You,
You let me choose.
So, I sit here and ask myself,
"What do you really want to do?"

I want to move in my sweet-spot.
My purpose here on earth.

I want to use my gifts for Your glory,
Surrendered to You King, for all I'm worth.

I'm thankful You care about me,
That's all that really matters.
So, I'm taking this day of rest Lord,
To go for a drive to hear Your voice above all the clatter.

I will go where You go.
I will stay where You stay.
I just want You Lord,
That's all that matters to my heart today.

109. I Remember You

August 13, 2016

I remember you.
It was about a year ago.
I doubt you remember me too,
We didn't even speak a word, I'm crazy, I know.

But why has God continuously placed you on my heart?
Do you need prayer?
Because that just seems to be my part,
In this world that needs even more prayer.

You know,
Sometimes God moves in the crazy.
I believe in faith if we Christians would go,
When God says "Go," we would not experience a life continuously hazy.

But our life would be clear,
With direction from our King.
Yes, we'd take crazy steps of faith,
But in that, life would not be overwhelming.

So, I've prayed for you.
Didn't really have the right words.
But God knew my genuine heart,
I just cared, as God whispered your true worth.

God loves His kids.
He will burden hearts.
We don't even have to know each other,
For God to move in a life, answering a sincere heart.

Sometimes in life the burdens get really heavy,
People tend to do that,
When they create yokes that aren't steady.
But God would never call you to do something petty.

He has a great plan for you.
I don't know you.
Seriously, know nothing about you.
I know I could have done some research, but I chose not to.

I simply sat and listened to God,
And what He told me about you.
That's how I wanted to pray,
God's words, not the world's way.

This is what the Lord whispered to my heart,
You are trustworthy, gifted at administration,
And you have a shepherd's heart.

Maybe one day I will talk to you,
But in the meantime, know I am praying for you.

Praying the Lord directs your steps,
And that God meets you right where you are with a word of encouragement.

110. Family

I have an amazing family,
Who loves me so much.
They have set such a high standard,
I'm afraid I will never meet a man who measures up.

I know there is a man out there,
Who will actually treat me tenderly and will care.
He won't take advantage of the gifts God has given me,
He will love me regardless, he will love our heirs.

He's out there.
I believe it.
I know other people have been raised well.
This man will know how to love me,
He knows I won't ring the bell.

Family dynamics are different.
I see it all around.
I'm used to my laid-back family.
We hang out at the beach for fun, we don't purposefully create battlegrounds.

Unless it's a nerf war.
Now that is fun.
Auntie busts out her gun,
And the boys know it's on.

As a sister,
I try to spoil my brothers.
I watch their kids whenever they need it,
So they can take their wives out with others.

And for my sister,
Love her dearly.
I've prayed and prayed for my sister,
And I love how God has blessed her sincerely.

As a daughter,
So blessed by my mom and dad.
Maybe it's because I'm the 4th kid,
But I'm so thankful they are not controlling or mad.

I can't wait to meet my future husband's family.
I've been praying for them too.
Praying **Matthew 5:1-16,**
Desiring they be blessed in all that they do.

Let your light so shine before men,
That they may see your good works,
And glorify your Father in heaven. (**Matthew 5:16**)

Praying they light up their world.
A city on a hill not hidden.
Blazing a trail for all the boys and girls,
Impacting all of the men and women.

All for the glory of God.
The only reason.
Knowing Jesus has died on the cross for all of us! (**John 3:16**)
And people need to hear it in this season.

Jesus is coming back.
We don't have time to slack.

Whatever our gifts are,
Praying we'd light up the dark.

Family is so important.
You're stuck with them for life.
But it's the best life,
With them by my side.

Why is it,
They know how to make me smile?
They just have this gift,
They always seem to go the extra mile.

I can't help laughing,
Call it a gift or something,
I won't ever stay sad,
Because they seriously are always up to something.

111. Amazing Love

August 15, 2016

Amazing Love,
Is a gift from above. (**James 1:17**)
We miss the meaning,
When we think we have to do something.
When isn't love,
A gift?

God gives the best gifts.
He knows how to bless His kids.
Have you received this gift?
This gift of love, Jesus Christ, is Him.

The Savior of our hearts,
He teaches us and shows us,
Who we truly are,
Loving us knowing we are but dust.

Beautiful things,
He creates.
He loves unconditionally,
His love never abates.

It's a gift.
Simply a gift.
And He's calling us to give gifts,
Unconditionally like Him.

God knows exactly what we need,
I think we know, too.
God provided for our needs,
When He commanded and told us what to do.

Beloved, let us love one another, (**1 John 4:7**)
For love is of God,
And everyone who loves is born of God,
And knows God.

He who does not love, (**1 John 4:8**)
Does not know God,
For God is love.

God is love! (**1 John 4:8**)
Jesus Christ is God. (**John 10:30**)
Jesus Christ is love!
And in His love,
He laid down His life for us,
Before we even said yes to His name, reigning above.

When we love unconditionally,
We meet the needs of those,
Who need to see Jesus entirely.

Reflecting Jesus in our actions,
Redeems our brother or sister,
Resetting the situation,
Remembering the gift love brings to one another.

It's a gift.
Simply a gift.

God gives us a gift,
When He allows us to give,
This amazing love,
Reflecting Jesus Christ who reigns above.

This indescribable gift,
We thank You God! **(2 Corinthians 9:15)**
For Jesus Christ is,
Amazing Love.

112. *Let's Build*

August 20, 2016

I want to live,
An altar building life,
Knowing Jesus already made,
The ultimate sacrifice.

An altar of worship,
Marking God's appearance, **(Genesis 12:7, 26:24-25)**

A time of remembrance, yet expectant,
A love for God's presence. (**Psalm 16:11**)

God has moved beyond our wildest dreams,
He's answered so many prayers,
The way He moves just seems,
To reveal He's there.

But He's not done moving,
There is more to do.
Jesus Christ will be returning,
So, let's pray expecting Him to accomplish what we can't do. (**Ephesians 3:20**)

Where two or three are gathered together,
In His name, He is there. (**Matthew 18:20**)
A promise.
He cares.

Jesus Christ made the ultimate sacrifice,
When he died a cruel and torturous death,
Giving up His life,
So, we could spend eternity in heaven as His Bride. (**Revelation 19:7**)

He lives to intercede for us. (**Hebrews 7:25**)
He is constantly praying.
He loves you personally,
So, cast your cares upon Him. (**1 Peter 5:7**)

An altar building life,
I want to live.
Constantly reminded,
Of the One who has shown me how to live.

We should never be too busy,
To build that altar and worship the Lord.

To get on our knees,
Praying and thanking Him in one accord.

Would we repent of our sin?
Seek Him,
And live,
Free from the bondage it causes within.

There is power in united prayer.
God hears.
He shows up there.

God's glory is seen in His church,
When His church humbles themselves,
Recognizing they are weak,
And they need His grace to be made well.

Whenever God appeared,
An altar was built. (**Genesis 12:7, 26:24-25**)
So, family,
Let's build.
Because He is here.

113. *True Father*

August 20, 2016

If people only talked to You,
They'd know.
You care about everything,
You are the True Father that desires for them to grow.

You don't hold them back.
Or mock them behind their back.
You sit and listen,
And share insights into Your Word that changes situations.

You know everything,
And yet You love it when we draw near.
You will hear every Word, (**1 Peter 5:7**)
Like a True Father who cares.

A True Father,
Listened to Hannah as she poured out her heart.
The priest didn't quite get it,
And condemned her, missing the anguish of her heart.

He didn't know the entire situation,
But her Father in heaven did,
And He answered her prayers,
And blessed her right in their midst.

Thank You Father,
For knowing exactly what we need,
Someone to walk with and talk to,
Someone who will listen to our pleas.

It's that knowledge of Your love,
Your caring heart.
Brings us to obedience in honor and respect,
Recognizing who You truly are.

You are Holy, Righteous, and Pure.
And yet You care for our world.
That amazes me, Father,
The fact that You bend down to hear my whispered word. (**Psalm 116:1-2**)

How can I honor You today?
Whom would You like for me to pray?
Thankful You know my heart,
You don't rate my prayers as if they were art.

Thank You King for knowing me,
For hearing my prayers,
For loving me.
You truly are all I need.

114. *Here to Serve*

August 20, 2016

Fill us with Your Holy Spirit, (**Acts 1:8**)
So, we can go out into all the world, (**Matthew 28:19**)
Wherever You place us Lord,
We are here to serve.

There is a flame of affection,
For You in our hearts.
You've sparked a fire,
We just want to be where You are.

Holy Spirit tell us where to go,
Make us sensitive to the need,
So, we can be the pure tool, (**2 Timothy 2:21**)
Jesus' hands and feet.

You've opened a door,
To the lost and the hurting.

Giving us the privilege to remind them,
Jesus is returning.

Jesus is returning.
Jesus is returning.

Fill us with Your Holy Spirit,
So, we can go out into all the world.
Thank You Lord for this gift,
We are here to serve.

115. Great Treasure

Psalm 119:133-140, 162
August 21, 2016

Direct my steps by Your word,
And let no iniquity have dominion,
Over me, Lord.
Redeem me from the oppression of man,
That I may keep Your precepts in this land.
Look down on me with love,
Make Your face shine,
As You teach me all Your principles from above.
Rivers of tears run down from my eyes,
Because people disobey Your law not seeking to be wise.
O Lord, You are righteous,
And Your decisions are fair.
Your decrees are perfect;
They are entirely worthy of our trust as we walk here.
My zeal has consumed me,
Because my enemies have disregarded Your Words stated clearly.

Your word is very pure;
Your promises have been thoroughly tested on earth.
That is why I love it.
I rejoice at Your word,
In awe of it.
As one who finds great treasure.

116. Where Does My Help Come From?

August 21, 2016

The righteous keep moving forward,
And those with clean hands,
Become stronger and stronger. (**Job 17:9**)

Clean hands and a pure heart,
Set people apart.
People will try to bring them down,
But their lies are unfound.

You can't argue with a life of integrity,
Not perfect, definitely human,
But seeking to live the Word of God entirely.

The Lord is the One who increases strength,
It's in His Word, a promise.
Those with clean hands will go the entire length.

I lift my eyes up to the hills, (**Psalm 121:1-2**)
Where does my help come from?
My help comes from—

The Lord!
Who made the heavens and the earth.

The Lord Himself watches over me,
He stands right beside me,
At my right hand. (**Psalm 121:5**)
Keeping me from all evil,
Preserving my life in this land. (**Psalm 121:7**)

117. *Psalm 119:153-161*

August 21, 2016

Look down upon my sorrows,
And rescue me.
For I have not forgotten Your law.
Plead my cause and redeem me,
Argue my case so they see.
Take my side,
Protect my life,
Give me back my life,
Just as You promised in Your Word for all eternity.

The wicked are far from salvation,
For they don't care about Your Word.
Great are Your tender mercies, O Lord,
In Your justice,
Give me back my life, so I can go into all the world.
Following Your guidelines revive me,
Even when many persecute and trouble me.
They are too many to count,
But why would I turn from Your testimony now?

I hate these traitors,
Because they care nothing for Your Word.
See how I love Your commandments Lord,
Out of Your life of love,
Prolong my life, so I can love.
All Your words are true,
Your righteous decisions are eternal.
Powerful people harass me without cause,
But my heart trembles only at Your Word.
I rejoice at Your Word,
As one who has found great treasure.

118. I Rise Early

August 21, 2016

I rise early,
Before the sun is up,
I cry out for help,
And put my hope,
In Your Word. (**Psalm 119:147**)

119. Keep Praying

August 21, 2016

I love the Lord,
Because He hears,
And answers my prayers.

Because He bends down and listens,
I will call upon Him as long as I live here. (**Psalm 116:1-2**)

And so I walk in the Lord's presence,
Here on earth as I live! (**Psalm 116:7**)
Jesus, You are my everything,
Your presence is a gift.

God hears.
He is near.
You are not alone.
He is standing right here.

He is bending down to hear,
Your very words.
You are His treasure.
You are His pearl.

Keep praying, friend,
Until the end.
Jesus is returning,
Keep praying, friend.
Keep praying.

120. Soul, Listen.

Soul,
Listen.
Forgive them.

Hear God speak to your heart,
Bless the Lord right where you are.

Rise to recover.
Stand and praise God like no other.

He hears you, He does.
He knows exactly what is going on as He sits above.

He knows and He is working in it.
You praise Him regardless of the unnecessary pain caused by it.

Jesus is with you.
He loves you.

Soul,
Listen.
Share Jesus' love with them.

121. King! We See You

King! We see You,
On Your throne, ready to make all things new.

While we bow here on earth,
Everything is a blur.

We see only You,
As we have one foot on earth yet one in heaven too.

Here we are Lord!
Send us out into the world!

We are ready to go,
Into all the world and sow.

Many seeds in Your name,
Wanting only to glorify the One who came.

To the earth to die for our shame,
Restoring us to a life that will never be the same.

We love You!
We just want to honor You!

Our desire Lord,
Is for those in all the world,

To know You, too.
To experience this life of Truth.

122. A Mission Until the End

Harvest Crusade, August 26-28, 2016
August 29, 2016

The Harvest Crusade,
Has come and gone.
So many lives met Jesus,
While we stood in awe.

Praising the Lord,
For His amazing grace.
Pouring out His love,
On this nation and every single race.

"Jesus loves you,"
Reached every heart.

Many left the stadium,
Ready to start.

To Follow the Lord,
Reading His word.
Praying and sharing,
And going to church.

Our prayer today,
Is that the seed fell on good soil,
And those who accepted the Lord,
Will grow in their walk, remaining loyal.

To our Savior Jesus Christ,
Who gave up His life,
Dying a cruel and tortuous death,
So we all can enjoy eternity in heaven.

Battling for lost souls is not easy,
It's a fight against the dark.
To live a life like you are in a life or death battle for souls,
Is a constant war.
So, I pray more.

From the lost to the saved,
Jesus touched each heart these days.
A mission until the end,
Jesus is returning, friend.

123. Worth It

As you pour out your heart,
To God in prayer-
Your praise, petitions, anxiety, anger or fear.

God hears you.
He loves you.
He will correct you,
Or He will encourage you.

God either corrects your wrong thinking,
Directing you by His Word to right thinking.
Or He encourages your heart to keep going,
Never quitting.

So, keep praying.
Never quit.
Keep praying, friend.
It's worth it.

124. Opportunities

Some people give people opportunities.
Other people ruin people so they never get an opportunity.

What type of person are you?
Remember, do unto others,
As you would have them do to you. (**Luke 6:31**)

125. Psalm 142

I cry out to the Lord with my voice,
With my voice,
To the Lord I make supplication.
I pour out my complaint,
Before Him,
Declaring all my troubles before Him.
For I am overwhelmed,
And You alone know me so well,
You know the path where I should walk.
Wherever I go, my enemies talk,
Setting traps for me.
I look for someone to come and help me,
But no one cares what happens to me.
They don't acknowledge me.
Refuge has failed me.
No one cares for my soul.
I cried out to You, O Lord, who knows my soul.
I say, "You are my place of refuge in this life.
You are all I want in life.
Hear my cry,
For I am very low, not high.
Rescue me from my persecutors,
For they are stronger.
Bring my soul out of prison,
So I can thank Your Son.
The godly will crowd around me,
For You treat me kindly."

126. When God Proves A Point

What do you do,
When God proves a point to you?

Repent, I pray.
And thank Him for allowing you to live another day.

God loves His kids.
He does.
He loves us regardless of the trials we face,
Knowing we don't get to choose our race.
But He loves us enough
To correct us when we are wrong.
He's not going to just agree,
Like everyone else does, who just go along.

Yes, when we face different trials,
God loves us regardless.
Sometimes when we experience a trial,
The enemy whispers, "God doesn't love you, that's obvious."

But that is a lie.
Even when we face great difficulty,
God loves us and watches us with His eye.
He steps in when it is too much for you or me.

But God will not agree with you,
When you yourself are wrong.
And your wrong action,
Has brought His people harm.

127. Love Is What Is Missing

Love is what is missing.
It's so obvious.
We think we know everything,
But we don't know how to practically "be."

Love the Lord your God,
With all your heart, soul, and mind.
Do you truly love God?
Do you walk in the fear of the Lord all of the time?

Love your neighbor as yourself.
Do you love your neighbor?
Or do you only love yourself?

What does it mean to truly love God?
It means we obey His Word.
Jesus is God and He said, (**John 10:30**)
"If you love Me, you'll obey My commandments," you'll obey what you
heard. (**John 14:15**)

Obedience is action.
Not just a thought or emotion.
It means we actively apply God's truths,
To our life in every situation.

It's our life.
It is what defines our life.
When we do something,
People should be able to read the Word by watching.

They may not know your action reveals a word from God.
But you know you are living the truth,
It's just what you do in life,
You actively seek to obey God with all your heart, soul, and your mind.

What does it mean to love your neighbor as yourself?
More often than not,
This is what is missing in a life obsessed with self.

Do we truly know how to love others,
In the way that meets their need?
Or are we only concerned with ourselves,
And what meets our own need?

Jesus gave a command,
That we love one another,
As He has loved us. (**John 15:12**)
In life, do we truly mimic His love?

Greater love has no one than this,
Than to lay down one's life for his friends. (**John 15:13**)
Why did Jesus give this command,
Unless He knew what we needed in the end?

Jesus knew the world would hate us, (**John 15:19**)
So, He said to all of us,
"Church, love each other,
Don't hate your brother." (**1 John 2:10-11**)

What do your actions show?
Love for one another,
Or do they actually show
Hate for your sister or brother?

When you lay down your life,
For your friend,
You give up something,
So, they will be better off in the end.

It's not about you.
Are you making their life miserable on purpose,
Because you want them to listen to you?
That's selfish and unloving and not what God wants.

This is tough love.
No, you're being tough because you don't know how to love.
You want your own way.
Admit it, that's why your stubborn will won't sway.

You are used to everyone agreeing,
And listening to you.
But oh wait,
Someone has brought up a point that has made you come unglued.

The world already hates us,
So why are you mimicking the world?
God never said, "throw your friend under the bus,
And watch them and see how they handle the hurt."

No, God said,
"You step in front of that bus,
And lay down your life for your friend.
You take the hit that was meant for them."

That's the love of a friend.
Jesus love,
That saves everyone from an unwanted end.
But how many know how to truly love?

It's obvious as one looks at the church in the world,
And sees more lust than love,
And they sit wondering what Jesus meant,
When He said, "Love."

Lust takes.
It watches.
Love gives.
It cares enough to step in.

Love steps into the picture,
Refusing to simply watch.
It enters a life,
Knowing love's true cause.

Love's true cause,
Is to mimic the life of Christ,
Who stepped in for us,
Dying so that we could have eternal life. (**John 15:13**)

The world is watching,
They don't know how to love.
They are watching you for an example,
Are you showing them God's true love?

128. *Fearless*

Fearless in the face of the one,
Who is supposed to be stronger.
I will stand.

Fearless in the face of the one,
Who is supposed to be wiser.
I will proclaim.

Fearless in the face of the one,
Who has been living longer.
I will remind.

Fearless in the face of the one,
Who should know the Word better.
I will edify.

For God has not given me a spirit of fear,
But of power, love, and a sound mind. (**2 Timothy 1:7**)
It's self- discipline.
God's kind.

God has chosen the foolish things of this world,
To put to shame those who think they are wise. (**1 Corinthians 1:27**)
He chose foolish weak me,
So, I guess He has a word for you, who are mighty and wise.

Let no one despise you for your youth,
But be an example to all the believers,
In word, conduct, in love,
In spirit, in faith, and in purity. (**1 Timothy 4:12**)

God will speak through anyone,
The humble will recognize that.
God is the One who appoints a person's work, (**John 3:27**)
He chose you for your job,
And me for mine.

129. Mention Jesus' Name

September 8, 2016

Whenever I'm struggling,
I mention Jesus' name,
To anyone standing by me,
They are all going to know He came.

He came and walked this earth,
Lived the life of a man.
Born of a virgin,
Died on the cross and rose again.

He died for our sins,
So that we could have the hope of heaven.
He took the penalty we deserved,
Because He loved us deep within.

Today, Jesus lives to intercede,
For you and me.
And whenever two or three
Are gathered in His name,
He joins and listens intently.

Every time I struggle,
And I start talking about Jesus,
I notice the struggle lesson,
As I remember how big Jesus is.

As I talk to whoever is next to me,
Really it doesn't matter who.
Every patient enters the conversation,
My coworkers too.

But even for them,
They mentioned they were encouraged.
They are facing different issues too,
And talking about Jesus brings constant assurance.

Assurance of a God who loves them,
And knows exactly what they are going through.
He knows every detail.
He knows what to do.

So, I encourage you today,
When you are struggling,
Just mention Jesus' name
And watch the demons flee.
Start talking about what you read,
In the Word,
What you learned at church,
Or what you overheard.

Just start talking about Jesus,
Knowing He will join the fun,
He will enter those within your circle,
And those struggling will remember that Jesus already won.

It's really amazing,
How the issue on your heart will leave.
So, the next time just mention Jesus' name,
And remind your friends of eternity.

It's His presence in your life,
That heals your heart.
No matter what you are going through, remember,
He cares and He knows exactly where you are.

130. *Truth Stands The Test Of Time*

September 9, 2016

Jesus wants His Bride to speak truth.
He hates lying. (**Proverbs 6:17**)
He hates deceit.
He died on the cross to deliver us from the power and effects of this
dishonesty.

Truth stands the test of time,
Lies are soon exposed. (**Proverbs 12:19 NLT**)
God knows the destructiveness of a lie,
Thus, He uncovers it and makes it known.

Lies breed a certain type of death,
Amongst those once close.
Death of a friendship.
Death of a relationship.
Death of trust.
Death of intimacy with the person you love the most.

Husbands and wives experience brokenness,
When they lie to one another.
Friends are no longer friends,
When they realize they can't trust each other.

From the beginning of the Bible,
To the end,
God has declared His love for Truth,
And His hatred for deceit which creates even more sin.

The damage it does,
Is more than some can even imagine.

That's why God hates it,
It is a no-win situation.

There is forgiveness, of course.
Jesus died on the cross for all of us.
However, it's not good enough to just have remorse.
Are you truly repentant?
Have you changed your course?

Prove by the way that you live,
That you have really turned from your sin (**Matthew 3:8**).
Have you turned to Christ?
Have you asked Him to forgive you of this struggle you have deep within?

Trust is born over time,
Once broken,
It takes time.
But it's not going to happen if you keep lying.

Trust is so key.
Will you ask your husband or wife for forgiveness today,
And restore your lost intimacy?
Will you forgive your husband or wife today,
Remembering Jesus loves them for eternity.

Unconditional love,
Is revealed in forgiveness.
Forgive your spouse today,
And experience God's grace.

Have you been hurt by someone who lied?
Truly hurt by the constant lies?
Will you forgive them today,
Even if they don't ask?
Obeying the Lord,
Forgetting the past.

Knowing God will speak to them,
And will deal with their heart the best.

131. What Should I do?

September 10, 2016

When my dreams,
Are not coming true,
Life is simply work,
And I'm way too far from you.
What should I do?

I have papers to write,
For school.
I have to work during my vacation,
Because I have to pay for things in life and for school.
Life is simply work,
And I'm way too far from you.

Yes, God is allowing me to use my gifts,
Right where I am at.
God is allowing others to read what I write,
They even can see me wear all of my hats.
But without you,
Life is simply work.
And I'm still way too far from you.

What girl doesn't want her man,
Sharing the land,
That God has given them both,

Making life a joy,
Not just work.

You're my other half,
Being far from you,
Kind of makes me mad.
Because you just have this gift,
Of always being able to make me laugh.
And I want to laugh,
Not be mad.
Especially when everyone around me is sad.
So without you,
Life is simply work,
Handsome,
I think I'm still way too far from you.

Where is the fun?
When you are missing the one
Who helps make life fun?

The only gift I want in life,
Is the grace of life.
Because then I will be spending life,
With my man,
That will be the best life,
Him holding my hand.

So when my dreams,
Are not coming true.
Life is simply work.
And I'm still way too far from you;
What should I do?

132. *Psalm 54*

September 10, 2016
Save me, O God,
By Your name.
Come with great power, O God,
And rescue me!
Defend me,
With Your might.
Hear my prayer tonight,
Pay attention to my plea.
For strangers are attacking me;
Violent men are trying to kill me;
Oppressors have sought after my life,
They care nothing for God in this life.
But God is my helper.
The Lord is with those who uphold my life.
May my enemies' plans for evil be turned against them?
Do as you promised and put an end to them.
I will freely sacrifice to You;
I will praise Your name, O LORD, for it is good.
For You will rescue me from my troubles,
And help me to triumph over my enemies.

133. *A Humbling Challenge*

September 10, 2016

A humbling challenge from the Lord.
Has God ever spoken to your heart,
Meeting you right where you are?

He knows your gifts,
He knows what you have faced.
Nothing deters Him,
He has a plan specifically for your race.

This race of life,
Led by God,
Is a sweet gift,
Solely because of God.

When Job's friends,
Accused him,
And constantly pointed fingers,
With no end.
Job did not yield,
He had not sinned.
But when God challenged Job,
Job was met deep within. (**Job 40**)

God's voice brought Job low.
Not man's voice.
God's voice supersedes every foe,
God's voice challenges and brings us low.

God knows everything,
While man only knows but a little.
God sees every need,
God will bring you to your knees.

Job's friends did not know,
That Satan was asking after Job.
All Job's friends saw,
Was the destruction, trying to figure out the cause.

But God knew,
Satan had to ask Him.

At the same time God knew Job's heart,
While he faced the constant accusation.

"Do you still want to argue with the Almighty?"
God asked Job.
With his hand over his mouth,
Job said "No."

"I know You can do anything,
And no one can stop You.
You ask, 'Who is this,
That questions My wisdom
With such ignorance?'
It is I, Job.
And I was talking about things,
I did not understand,
Things to wonderful for me,
I take back everything I said.
I had heard you before,
But now I see You with my own eyes,
I sit in dust and ashes wanting to cry."

When Job prayed for his friends,
The Lord restored his fortunes.
God gave him twice as much as before,
God restored.

God dealt with Job's friends.
In fact, God was angry
With their constant accusation.

God had a word for each life.
And that's a word for our life.
God knows where He wants you spiritually,
And so, He will allow certain things to happen to you and me.

You also never know the spiritual battle,
Taking place.
So often our eyes are blurred,
We only see what is right in front of our face.

God has a humbling challenge,
For you and me,
Do you hear Him saying to you today,
"Do you still want to argue with the Almighty?"

134. *Chase Grace*

September 12, 2016

Don't forget grace.
Don't let grace get away.
Chase grace.

For by grace,
We have been saved,
Through faith in Jesus Christ. (**Ephesians 2:8**)
This is the life.

Salvation brings God glory,
Showcasing His love, mercy—
His- story. (**Ephesians 2:4-6**)

Freeing people from the power,
And effects of sin,
By Jesus Christ's death,
And resurrection.

Once dead,
Now alive,
Free to live,
This life in Christ.

Grace in its love,
Doesn't hide,
Covers our sin with blood,
So, we can have eternal life. (**1 Peter 4:8**)

Never forget,
The gift of life.
Freely given,
The Ultimate Sacrifice.

The beauty of this grace displayed,
His kindness in saving sinners every day,
Brings God eternal glory,
As He showcases to the world, His- story. (**Ephesians 2:7**)

Grace redeems.
Grace truly sees you and me.
The law condemns, (**Romans 3:20**)
Grace sets you free.

Don't forget grace.
Don't let grace get away.
Chase grace.

135. A Ruler

September 12, 2016

A ruler who lacks understanding,
Is a cruel oppressor.
But he who hates unjust gain,
Will prolong his days for forever. (**Proverbs 28:16**)

It's a matter of the heart,
The Lord pointing out,
Exactly where you are.

Are you going to hold someone down,
So, you can take ground?
Or are you going to set them free,
So, your nation can continue to be?

136. When I Remember

September 12, 2016

When I remember,
I will choose to forget.
I won't replay that hurt,
Over and over in my head.

That hurt in the past,
Takes from today.
It's so present sometimes,
But I choose to not be swayed.

I will talk to You Lord,
And hear Your voice.
For Your voice covers my pain,
I choose to rejoice.

I will rejoice in You,
For You are my refuge.
My Rock and my Salvation,
My Deliverer from oppression.

Draw near to my soul,
And redeem it!
Deliver me, Lord,
I need it! (**Psalm 69:18**)

137. God Has Given You A Gift

September 13, 2016

God has given you a gift,
But He's not done growing you,
In your gift.

Ask Him in prayer,
Listen with a fine tune ear,
To what He's whispering to your heart,
Wait to hear His heart.

We experience true peace,
In God's presence.
For He remains in control,
His love for you is unconditional.

God loves you so much.
He has a plan.
Wait and listen, friend,
His plan is more than you can even imagine.

What do you think,
God is calling you to do?
Ok, don't do it,
Unless you have to!

If you can't hold back,
It's like fire burning in your bones,
You have to share Jesus,
In this way so others will know.

Then that's what God wants you to do.
It's the burden He's placed on your heart.
That is where God wants you to start.

And as you obey,
Listening to God each day,
Doing what He's calling you to do,
You will light a path so others can follow you.

It's a gift,
Being able to reach out to others,
With Jesus Christ on our lips.

Jesus personally made sure heaven,
Is in your story,
You have the assurance that He wants you impacting others saying,
"Friend, God wants you in glory."

So, my prayer for you today,
Is that God will whisper to your heart,

And you will hear Him saying,
"Daughter, I'm going to turn your scars into stars."

138. I Believe In You

September 13, 2016

I believe in you.
Do you believe in me?

I know God has given you a gift to use.
You're not meant to be held down,
But to take ground for God's glory.

139. I Need You

September 14, 2016

My proud and angry heart,
Doesn't fit with who You are.
My struggle remains,
Why can't I change?

I'm fine,
And then I'm not.
It's like a light switch,
That flips.

I don't know what to do,
Lord, please, I need You.
I need You to whisper to my heart,
I need You to remind me of who You are.

I need a new heart,
For the one I have is cold.
I need You to take out this heart of stone, (**Ezekiel 36:26**)
And give me a heart of flesh that You can hold.

Whenever I remember,
The struggle surfaces,
How do I deal with these memories,
Of being so hurt?

I'm not godly,
Not like those saints.
I just can't seem to brush this off,
For I was changed.

It affected my life,
No one else seemed to care.
They go on living their life,
While I struggle trying to move forward from here.

I love You Lord,
I just want to honor You.
It's that fear of disappointing You,
That makes me want a heart that is new.

Forgive me Lord,
For not handling this well.
I love You Lord,
Please make all things new! (**2 Corinthians 5:17**)

140. Keep Moving Forward, Friend

September 16, 2016

God knew today would happen,
It's written in His book. (**Psalm 139:16**)
Keep moving forward, friend,
Believe me, you are not overlooked.

God knows you.
He loves you.
He has a plan.
Keep moving forward, friend,
Endure to the end.

God's given you His Word.
Those sweet words of truth.
The wisdom He shares,
Guards your steps,
Making all things new.

He restores the years, (**Joel 2:25**)
The locust have eaten.
He hears your every prayer.
He knows the needs of men and women,
He will burden your heart to intercede for many this year.

So look straight ahead, (**Proverbs 4:25**)
And fix your eyes on what is before you.
Don't worry or fear,
Soon you will hear a voice behind you, (**Isaiah 30:21**)
Saying, "This is the way, turn and walk here."

Mark out a straight path for your feet, (**Proverbs 4:26**)
Then stick to the path and stay safe.
Anchor yourself in God's Word,
Remembering, God's promises will always remain.

Above all else guard your heart, (**Proverbs 4:23**)
For it affects everything you do.
God loves your heart, friend.
Keep guarding what God has entrusted to you.

Never let loyalty and kindness get away from you! (**Proverbs 3:3-4**)
Wear them like a necklace,
Write them deep within your heart.
Don't lose your grip on Love,
And you will find favor
Earning a good reputation near and far.

So, keep moving forward, friend,
Keep moving forward.
Cling to God's Word,
Intercede in prayer,
Share His love,
Be planted in the church,
And you will grow mightily this year!

141. 70x7

September 17, 2016

Seventy times seven, (**Matthew 18:22**)
He's called us to forgive.
Seventy times seven,
Releases us from overwhelming burdens.

God knows.
He knows we are but dust. (**Psalm 103:14**)
He knows our needs.
He calls us to trust. (**Proverbs 3:5-6**)

He calls us to trust Him,
When He says,
"Seventy times seven you are to forgive."
Yes, trust Him,
Even when it hurts to forgive.

Sometimes you feel taken advantage of,
And then that whispered thought,
"If I forgive them,
They are just going to do this again, unless they're taught,
A lesson."

But who is the Teacher?
You or God?
Are you wiser than the Almighty?
Did you create the earth with one spoken word?

You are not God.
You are His servant.
You are living and breathing today,
Because He spoke one word.

You are not the One in control.
You do not know everything.
You do not know what they need to reach spiritual maturity,
In fact, you do not even know what you yourself need entirely.

Seventy times seven, (**Matthew 18:22**)
He's called us to forgive.
Seventy times seven,
Because He knows what we need.

"If you love Me, you'll obey Me." (**John 14:15**)
The Lord Jesus Christ says.
Do you love Jesus?
Will you forgive every day?

Seventy times seven, (**Matthew 18:22**)
He's called us to forgive.
But have you asked for forgiveness yet,
So that you can live,
Free from the guilt and shame,
That weighs a person down,
With self-blame?

Jesus Christ knows what we need,
To live guilt free.
Thus, He's given us His Word,
If only we'd come up under.

And recognize He's All-Knowing,
He knows our every need.
And while we all walk this earth,
He wants us to grow in spiritual maturity.

142. Broken

September 18, 2016

Someone needs to be fed,
So, God is going to break you,
For when you are broken,
Many are fed through you.

They are hungry,
And needy too.
Don't worry.
God is with you,
He will feed you,
As you go through.

His presence in your life,
Feeds your soul.
Point them to Jesus,
Your joy bucket is full.

Sometimes the greatest fruit in our lives,
Is born out of affliction.
We may not see it with our eye,
But when we are broken,
And on our knees, weak in the world's eyes,
Weak before Christians,
God uses us in powerful ways,
To meet the needs,
That otherwise would not have been met this day.

This is not purposeless,
God loves you too much.
His end game is for you to be more like Jesus,
Who was broken for us.

143. Didn't Even Have To Hide

September 20, 2016

"Daniel, servant of the living God, (**Daniel 6:20**)
Has your God,

Whom you serve continually,
Been able to provide a delivery,
From the lions who seek you so ferociously."

Yes. (**Daniel 6:22**)
He never left my side.
He sent His angel to shut the lions' mouths,
I didn't even have to hide.

I was found innocent before Him, (**Daniel 6:22**)
And, O king,
I have done you no wrong,
So why have you caused this suffering?

Why did you believe those men?
Who lied again and again.
They were jealous,
And selfish,
They just wanted your attention,
So, they made up this mess.

God knew.
And so He protected me,
From your crew,
That needs to learn how to "flee."

144. God's Glory

September 20, 2016

When Ezekiel saw God's glory,
He fell on his face. (**Ezekiel 1:28**)

When Isaiah saw God's glory,
He said, "Woe is me, I'm a sinful man and a member of a sinful race."
(**Isaiah 6:5**)

When you see God's glory,
What do you do?
Are you changed?
Or unmoved?

145. *As A Family*

September 20, 2016

King Jesus, as a family,
We honor You.
With our life,
We submit to You.

We seek to say,
Only what You call us to say.
Dying to ourselves,
Saying, "Have Your way."

Your Word is truth,
May that be the word on our lips.
Sharing with others,
Jesus Christ alone saves, providing eternal bliss.

Jesus, You are returning,
It is closer than we can even imagine.
Would Your church be ready, Lord,
Seeking to reach the lost with the gospel until the end.

146. God Has Not Forgotten You

September 20, 2016

God has not forgotten you!
Believe it!
He will deliver you.
His timing is perfect for it.

God has placed you right where you are,
For such a time as this.
God has given you this position for a reason,
So take a risk.

He knows what you are facing,
He sees your heart.
He knows everyone around you,
Better than they even realize, thus far.

God has not forgotten you!
Believe it!
He will deliver you.
His timing is perfect for it.

God's delivery will impact,
More than you know.
He knows what is needed,
This is not just for show.

He cares about eternity,
And the destination of all.
There is a heaven and a hell,
It is our choice where we go.

He wants people to choose heaven,
But some are blind.
They need to hear His words of truth,
So He sent you to a place where you'd reach their mind.

He knows how they will receive it,
So yes, He's allowed this.
You are a pure tool He's chosen to use, (**2 Timothy 2:21**)
To reach the hearts and minds with the gospel news.

God has not forgotten you!
Believe it!
He knows what is best for you.
So He will deliver you perfectly from this.

147. *Close*

September 23, 2016

Moments when I've asked,
"Why?"
And I knew Lord,
You heard my faint cry.

You didn't have to answer,
I knew that,
But You didn't object to me asking,
You listened, keeping my heart intact.

Moments when I faintly heard,
Your whispered words.

As I leaned in intently,
Reading Your Word.

"I want you close to Me,"
You said.
As I read Your Words,
In John 10.

As the Shepherd of the sheep,
You, Jesus, know exactly how to keep,
Us safe from harm,
You see what we need,
You are the alarm.

You want us close,
And You know exactly what it will take,
You care too much,
Our souls are at stake.

There is a very real enemy,
Who wants to snatch Your own.
But You've put Your foot down,
Keeping us close, saying "No."

Safe in the Shepherd's arms,
We are.
You keep us close,
To keep our souls safe from harm.

We will face different things,
Trials and suffering,
But in those moments I will remember,
I am close to my King.

148. You See My Reflection

September 23, 2016

Jesus, You see my reflection,
My reflection to the world.
Lord, I want to reflect You,
Even when I'm struggling to be that godly girl.

As a face is reflected in water,
So the heart reflects a person. (**Proverbs 27:19 NLT**)
When they see my heart, Lord,
Will they see You or will they only make fun?

Will they constantly search for a fault?
Wanting to only tear down,
Or make themselves feel better,
Never even wanting me around.

Do they just want something,
Not caring that I'm a human?
When they see my heart, Lord,
Will they see You or will they only make fun?

Jesus, You see my reflection,
My reflection to the world.
What do You see Jesus,
Do You see a godly girl?

Lord, I want to reflect You,
But I am not perfect.
Thank You for dying for my sin,
Thank You for making me look perfect.

It's You Lord,
Did they miss that fact?
You are the One that strengthens us,
Giving us the boldness and courage to speak with tact.
Any perfection people may see,
Is You covering what we lack.

You strengthen us in our weakness,
You've given us everything we need.
Those watching and analyzing,
Should probably, instead, get on their knees.

Jesus, You see my reflection,
My reflection to the world.
I just want to reflect You, Jesus,
Being bold, sharing the gospel to all the lost in the world.

This side of heaven,
I want my heart to reflect You.
Those sweet moments when You give us a choice,
"How are you going to handle this news?"

In heaven,
When I look You in the face,
Lord Jesus I pray,
My expression reflects Yours that day!

As a face is reflected in water, (**Proverbs 27:19 NLT**)
So the heart reflects a person.
When they see my heart, Lord,
Will they see You or will they only make fun?

149. *Called To Liberty*

September 23, 2016

The need for freedom,
Comes from within.
"You have been called to liberty, brethren." (**Galatians 5:13**)

The freedom to make your own choices,
Though not "using liberty,
As an opportunity for the flesh"
But to experience the life of Christ who came in the flesh.

You shall know the truth,
And the truth shall make you free.
Jesus Christ is truth,
Jesus Christ has set you free.

You once were slaves of sin,
Now you are free in Christ.
You would have experienced eternal death,
Now you experience eternal life.

The Son has set you free,
You are free indeed.
Free from bondage,
Free from anxiety.

Free to move in your sweetspot,
Not being held down,
Free to move with confidence,
Using your spiritual gifts without bounds.

150. *The Impact Of My Sin*

September 24, 2016

If I saw the impact of my sin,
On those around me;
Would my heart tremble at that bad decision?
Or would I walk away undeterred by all those struggling?

151. *Freedom to Choose*

September 24, 2016

If you feel like your freedom,
Has been taken away.
Remember, Christian,
One freedom remains.

The freedom to choose your attitude,
Toward any given situation,
Is a freedom Jesus Christ gives, (**2 Corinthians 3:17**)
That allows us to reflect His image. (**Romans 8:29, 2 Corinthians 3:18**)

152. Repent Today

September 25, 2016

God has blessed you with so much,
He'd give you even more.
And yet you took,
From the one who is poor. (**2 Samuel 12**)

The poor man had nothing,
Except for this one thing.
It was a gift from God,
But to you that didn't mean anything.

You took it like you owned it,
When God didn't give it to you.
You acted like you did nothing,
You covered your sin, but God saw you.

You couldn't take some time,
Using your own resources.
If you had only prayed to God first,
He would have answered you and blessed. (**2 Samuel 12:7-8**)

Why have you despised the commandment of the Lord, (**2 Samuel 12:9**)
To do evil in His sight?
That did not belong to you,
Yet you took it, not expecting a fight.

You are not above God,
He's the One that has given you your position.
Repent today,
Recognizing the One who is on the throne and in control of this situation.

God will deal with you,
For there are repercussions for sin.
Yes, God forgives you when you ask,
He's waiting for you to say, "I have sinned."

You need a Savior,
The Lord Jesus Christ.
To rescue you from your sinful nature,
Giving you the desire to be more like Christ.

Be thankful for Christ's death,
On the cross that day.
For His one act,
Took away all of your guilt and shame.

He will fill you with His Holy Spirit,
When you ask Him each day.
He will help you to resist temptation,
When you remain surrendered to Him day by day.

It is by His power alone,
Not yours.
That You will be able to walk this journey,
Resisting the temptations of the world.

153. A Leader vs. A Controlling Person

October 1, 2016

What is the difference,
Between leading and control?
A leader guides and points to Jesus,
While a controlling person seeks authority above all.

A leader is a servant,
Serving and instructing.
Knowing Jesus said, "The first shall be last and the last first," (**Mark 10:31**)
The word— "We've come to serve not be the ones taking."

A controlling person does not listen,
They only hear their own voice,
They want people to always listen,
To their choice.

A controlling person constantly tells people what to do,
They do not leave room for growth,
But again, want the power and authority,
Holding people down because they constantly don't hear but say "no."

A leader allows one to grow in their gift,
They guide and point to Jesus in His Word,
Knowing that wisdom and knowledge,
Supersedes the wisdom of man in this world.

Jesus was a leader,
He laid down His life for us,
He wanted us to enjoy the abundant life,
So, He took the hit meant for us.

A leader takes responsibility,
And desires to handle things well,
Seeking Jesus' guidance in the Word,
Ready whether in or out of season to tell.

All those needing to see Jesus,
In their specific situation,
Desiring biblical conflict resolution,
Needing to see God's glory in this specific season.

154. *Peace*

October 1, 2016

What does peace look like?
Jesus says, "Peace I leave with you,
My peace I give to you;
Not as the world gives do I give to you.
Let not your heart be troubled,
Neither let it be afraid." (**John 14:27**)
This is the peace Jesus gives to you today.

It's a gift.
Peace.
A gift from Jesus.
Something He leaves.

Peace amongst people.
What does that look like?
Is it seen in forgiveness?
Or fake smiles and a prolonged fight?

155. *Advice*

October 2, 2016

Everyone seems to want to give advice,
They want to speak into your life.
They want the authority,
They want you to listen,
They want the power,
They think you should do this then.

How do people react,
When you don't take their advice?
Do they simply say, "ok,"
Or do they argue thinking you are the one unwise?

How do you react,
When others don't take your advice?
Really, are you thinking of what's good for them,
Or are you only thinking of yourself and what's best for your own life.

Be careful who you listen to,
It's your life.
You will be held accountable by Jesus,
For the decisions you made with this gift called life.

What is the best advice given?
Advice that comes straight from the Word.
Who cares about man's opinion,
I want Jesus' words.

156. Seek God Consistently

October 2, 2016

If you are not seeking God consistently,
In His Word;
You will be washed to and fro,
By man's unconventional words.

When you are filled with the Holy Spirit,
You will sense that heart-check,

"Don't listen to this,
Go over there instead."

God knows Satan wants to infiltrate our mind,
Because Satan wants control.
But when you submit yourselves to God in His Word,
The enemy has absolutely no control.

Guard your mind,
Guard what you think,
Guard your heart,
For it affects everything. (**Proverbs 4:23**)

God wants the best for you,
He does have a great plan.
But there is an enemy out there,
That wants to keep you from the abundant life in this land.

When those unwanted words come,
Maybe it's someone trying to get you to do something,
Or even an unwanted involuntary thought that makes you come undone,
Pray in the moment seeking—

Whatever things are true
Whatever things are noble
Whatever things are just
Whatever things are pure
Whatever things are lovely
Whatever things are of a good report
If there is any virtue
And if there is anything praiseworthy
Meditate on these things. (**Phil. 4:8**)

It's seeking God in the moment,
Asking Him to take control.

He will help you handle the situation,
For He is Lord over all.

157. Trust God's Heart

October 2, 2016

Trust God's heart,
He's with you in this.
He's whispering words to your soul,
You won't want to miss.

Be still and know,
It may come in the breeze.
But don't forget to look for the fire,
Blazing amongst all the trees.

He's constantly talking,
Did you catch it?
His word for your heart,
Did you miss it?

He loves you so much,
His presence is so near.
Trust God's heart,
Don't fear.

158. *Look Up and See*

October 2, 2016

On my knees,
Praying this day.
I look up and see,
His face shining my way. (**Psalm 67:1**)

"What do you want?"
His whispered word comes.
A blessing from You, Lord,
Is all I want.

You've given me land.
I love it so much.
But Lord, may I have springs of living water? (**Joshua 15:18-19**)
I need Your touch.

Your touch on my life,
Filling me with the Holy Spirit.
For it's Your power Lord,
That allows something to reach everyone who needs it.

That's all I want.
To be used by You.
My life is Yours,
Please anoint it so it reaches a few.

On my knees,
Praying this day.
I look up and see,
His face shining my way. (**Psalm 67:1**)
Saying, "Yes, I'll fill you today!"

159. Give Thanks

October 2, 2016

Oh, give thanks to the LORD!
Call upon His name;
Make known His deeds among the peoples,
Sing to Him, sing psalms to Him, (**1 Chronicles 16:8-9a**)
Praise His name!

Talk of all His wondrous works!
Glory in His holy name;
Let the hearts of those rejoice who seek the Lord! (**1 Chronicles 9b-10**)
Praise His name!

Seek the Lord and His strength;
Seek His face evermore!
Remember His marvelous works which He has done,
His judgments and yes, all His wonders. (**1 Chronicles 16:11-12**)

Praise His name!
Glory in His holy name!
No matter what you're facing today,
Give to the LORD the glory due to His name. (**1 Chronicles 16:29a**)

Sweet sacrifice,
A worshipful heart.
No matter what you are facing,
Come, God loves your heart.

Oh, Worship the Lord,
In the beauty of holiness. (**1 Chronicles 16:29b**)
Praise His name,
And your soul will be blessed.

160. You Do Not Need to Fight

October 2, 2016

You do not need to fight this battle, (**2 Chronicles 20:17**)
Victory is already yours.
Position yourself on your knees,
Keeping your eyes on the Lord.

Tomorrow, go out against them,
Do not fear or be dismayed,
For the Lord is with you, (**2 Chronicles 20:17**)
He will defeat your enemies this day.

We bow our heads,
Face to the ground,
Bowed before the Lord,
Worshipping Him now. (**2 Chronicles 20:18**)

The children stand,
With voices loud and high,
Singing to the Lord,
Throughout the night. (**2 Chronicles 20:19**)

Rising early the next day,
Believing in the Lord,
Those appointed to sing,
Sang songs to the Lord. (**2 Chronicles 20:20-21**)

The beauty of holiness,
Walking before the army praising His holy splendor,
Singing, "Give thanks to the Lord,
His faithful love endures forever." (**2 Chronicles 20:21**)

161. *Thankful*

October 2, 2016

I'm thankful for those times,
People I didn't even know,
Were nice.

It convicts my heart,
Because there are times,
I struggle with reaching out.

They have no idea,
The impact they have,
Moments when my words don't come,
But stay in my head.

God knows my heart,
Thankful for that.
So, I pray for those who are nice,
I pray God's face shines.

"God be merciful to them and bless them,
And cause Your face to shine upon them.
That Your way may be known on earth,
Your salvation among all the men and women." (**Psalm 67:1-2**)

You know their heart, Lord,
Reach them where they are.
Praying they experience the fullness of joy in Your presence, (**Psalm 16:11**)
Thank You, King, for their caring heart.

162. *Do What Is Right*

October 3, 3016

"For the LORD God is a sun and shield;
The LORD will give grace and glory;
No good thing will He withhold
From those who walk uprightly." (**Psalm 84:11**)

Do what is right,
In the eyes of the LORD.
Honor Him with your conduct,
And impact those in your world.

The LORD is a Light,
Shining the way.
Also, a Protector,
Shielding you from the evil today.

He will give grace,
And glory to His own.
Reach out to the lost,
And receive a crown.

163. *fruit*

October 3, 2016

there is fruit in the valley
there is
but you don't hold a person down
just so you get fed

for what if
there is greater fruit
if you lift them up
and hear the truth

for what if
God has a word for you
but you won't hear that word
if you don't do what God has already called you to do

164. Don't Be Unequally Yoked

October 3, 2016

Don't be unequally yoked,
God has a plan.
Wait and seek God,
And in His perfect timing you'll meet your man.

It may take forever,
But that's ok.
Jesus is so faithful,
To hold your heart at bay.

When you wait and serve God,
With your gifts,
He will bring you the right man,
That fits.

Don't try and make things work,
Or cling too tight to what's wrong,

Wait for God,
And seek Him in His Word.

It is difficult,
I know.
The struggle is real.
For sure.

But worth it.
When it's the right one,
Don't just try and make things work,
Wait for God's chosen one.

See, here's the thing,
You want to be equally yoked,
So, you move forward together in God's perfect timing.

Because God has a plan.
But if you are too far ahead of your man,
All you're going to do is stand,
Waiting for him to catch up to God's plan.

But hear this too,
If that godly man is too far ahead of you,
Girl step it up,
Or you will hold him back too.

Also, you have to find him so hot!
Go ahead and laugh,
But believe me you'll thank me when you tie the knot.

It's biblical.
It is.
But don't forget this
He needs to be your best friend above everyone else.

He's the one you want to talk to all of the time,
The one you want to gain wisdom from,
The one you can't imagine life without,
He's the only one you can picture being the father to your daughters and sons.

So, moving forward together spiritually,
He's a hottie,
And your best friend,
Totally worth it in the end.

Looks will fade,
As will your memory and even your brain,
But that best friend and your heart before the Lord,
Will remain.

Wait for it
It's worth it.
Just wait girl,
God will bless you for it.

165. Living Life Forgiven

October 4, 2016

Living life forgiven,
Refusing to give up,
Remembering redemption,
And His relentless love.

Receiving His grace,
His relentless love,
Shines on my face.

He doesn't give up,
But chases after me,
Jesus Christ,
Won't let me flee.

He keeps me close,
So that I can boast,
Of His relentless love,
A gift from above.

The blood of Christ,
Paid my price.
Eliminating death,
Saving my life.

He's relentless,
Everyday regardless.
Relentless,
While I'm speechless.
Relentless,
When I feel worthless.
Relentless,
Even as I write this.

His relentless love,
Washes over my face,
Freeing me from disgrace,
And the humiliation I face.

Not giving up,
But loving me when I'm weak,
His relentless love,
Flows through eternity.

166. The Vision You Have

October 4, 2016

O Lord my God,
I cried out to you,
And you healed me, (**Psalm 30:2**)
So that I could see,
The vision You have,
For those You want in heaven's eternity.

I was blind to their suffering,
Then You opened my eyes.
I was crying because I failed to see,
The destruction caused by all of their lies.

You broke through the silence,
To give me a word,
Many were hurting,
Because I hadn't said a word.

Forgive me Lord,
For my words unsaid,
Thank You for opening my eyes,
To the vision You have.

Valley's bring vision,
Often caused by a broken heart,
Here I am Lord,
This is tearing me apart.

I'll go where You want me,
I will simply repeat Your words.
Forgive me for my hesitancy,
I'm all Yours.

167. Victory Magnifies God

October 5, 2016

Victory magnifies God,
As His deliverance impacts the world.
It comes from Him,
It glorifies Him,
It honors Him,
Victory reveals His Sovereign control.

Victory comes from You, O Lord,
May Your blessings rest on your people. (**Psalm 3:8**)
Thank You for reaching our world,
Your love displayed in the death of Your Son is unstoppable.

168. Arm Yourselves

October 5, 2016

Arm yourselves Christians,
For the fight.
Don't back down,
Get on your knees tonight.

See the vision,
Spend more time in prayer.
Pray and intercede,
Battling today for all of your heirs.

Today matters,
It's an appointed time in space,

God placed you here,
Get on your face.

Battling for lost souls,
Is not easy.
It's a fight against the dark.
Arm yourselves Christian,
This is war.

You must endure hardship,
As a good soldier of Jesus Christ.
You will face different types of suffering,
But God's hand is on your life.

He knows your tomorrows,
So, He is preparing you today.
He is in control of your life,
Sit still and see the revelation of Jesus Christ.

169. Own Up

October 6, 2016

own up to your mistake
don't brush it under the rug
it will just resurface
if it wasn't taken care of.

170. Will You Obey

October 6, 2016

What has God already told you to do?
Will you obey today?
He loves you so much please trust His heart—
"Yes Lord, have Your way."

171. God Will Restore

October 6, 2016

God will restore the years
The locust have eaten. (**Joel 2:25**)
He will heal your heart.
His timing is perfect,
Trust His strong arm.

172. Pray For Another Chance

October 6, 2016

When you feel like you missed an opportunity,
Again.
What do you do?
But pray for another chance, again.

Moments when God says,
"I already told you what to do."
And moments when I cry out,
"Who in the world is it that I haven't talked to?"

Maybe I should start looking,
To the right or to the left.
But I thought God told me,
To look straight ahead.

There was no one in front of me,
I smiled at those that were,
I'm working on this friendliness thing,
It's just taking me a little bit of time, unlike before.

I love You Lord,
And I'm thankful for the second and third chance.
I do believe You just might have given me a word like Jonah,
I just don't want to end up in the whale's belly because I would lose my tan.

173. Love Displayed

October 7, 2016

Love displayed,
His blood forgave,
Every sin of man,
Repent and be forgiven.

174. The Cross Shone

The cross shone,
People wept,
A perfect man,
Died for them.

175. Seeing the Cross

It is by seeing the cross
And those around—
The sinner's eyes are opened
Once lost, now is found.

Unity speaks
It's a crowd shouting out.
We are forgiven and free,
Come experience life free of doubt.

176. Jesus' Arms

October 8, 2016

When you feel exposed,
And you just want a safe haven,
Run to the cross,
Jesus' arms are open.

Jesus' arms,
Will keep you safe from harm.
From those who just exploit,
But do nothing to protect you in this spiritual war.

Your life,
Means so much to Him.
Run to Jesus,
He's your Refuge from all the women and men.

He cares for you.
He loves you.
He is your safe haven,
From the world's constant view.

They will watch,
They will talk,
But Jesus will move,
And actively protect you.

No weapon formed against you will prosper, (**Isaiah 54:17**)
While Jesus is your Defender.
Safe in His arms,
You are protected from the world's harm.

Safe haven's home,
Is found in Jesus' arms.
The BEST Protector,
In this constant spiritual war.

177. Sit Before God

October 8, 2016

When I sit before God in the morning,
And read,
He speaks to me.

I sit and hear His voice,
Speaking into my life,
Telling me to make the right choice.

Today He said,
"I have prepared you,
For what's ahead.
It's bigger than you know,
More than you can even imagine.
My hand is on you, though,
So, go into all the world and share these words I've said":

The Lord is my Rock,
My Fortress,
My Savior,
My Deliverer.
The God in whom I find protection,
From the world. (**2 Samuel 22:2-3**)

God is bedrock under my feet,
The castle in which I live,
My rescuing knight.
My God, where I run for dear life. (**2 Samuel 22:2-3**)

I sing to God,
And find myself safe and saved. (**2 Sam 22:4**)
Safe from my enemies,
As waves of death surrounded me. (**2 Sam 22:4-5**)

All of the ungodliness,
Made me afraid. (**2 Sam 22:5b**)
But I was safe,
With the One who stayed.

In fear and distress,
I called out to the Lord for help.
From His palace on high
He heard my cry,
And brought me right into His presence,
With Him—A private audience. (**2 Samuel 22:7**)

Then the earth shook and trembled,
The foundations of heaven were shaken,
Because He was angry, (**2 Samuel 22:8**)
With them.

The Lord thundered from heaven,
The Most High gave a mighty shout.
He shot His arrows and scattered His enemies,
He hurled his lightnings—a rout! (**2 Sam 22:14-15**)

The secret sources of ocean were exposed,
The hidden depths of earth lay uncovered,
At the rebuke of the Lord,
He let loose His hurricane anger. (**2 Sam 22:16**)

He reached down from heaven,
And rescued me,
He pulled me out of the ocean of hate,
That enemy chaos which was drowning me. (**2 Sam 22:17**)

They hit me when I was down,
But God stuck by me. (**2 Sam 22:19**)
They attacked me at a moment when I was weakest,
But the Lord upheld me. (**2 Sam 22:19**)

He led me to a place of safety,
He rescued me because He delights in me. (**2 Sam 22:20**)
I stood there saved—
Surprised to be loved! (**2 Sam 22:20**)

The Lord rewarded me for doing right,
God made my life complete,
He compensated me because of my innocence,
For I have kept the ways of the Lord, instead of turning to evil from He.
(**2 Sam 22:21-22**)

I am blameless before God;
I have kept myself from sin.
The Lord rewarded me for doing right,
Because of my innocence in His sight. (**2 Sam 22:24-25**)

God rewrote the text of my life,
When I opened the book of my heart to His eyes. (**2 Sam 22:25**)
You stick by people who stick with you.
You're straight with people who're straight with you. (**2 Sam 22:26**)

To the faithful,
You show yourself faithful.
To those with integrity,
You show integrity.
To the pure,
You show yourself pure.
But to the wicked,
You show yourself hostile instead. (**2 Sam 22:26-27**)

You rescue those who are humble,
But Your eyes are on the proud to humiliate them. (**2 Sam 22:28**)
Oh Lord, I need You,
To rescue me from them.

Oh Lord, You are my light,
Yes, Lord, You light up my darkness. (**2 Sam 22:29**)
Your way is perfect, (**2 Sam 22:31a**)
Every God-direction is road-tested,
Everyone who runs toward Him makes it. (**2 Sam 22:31**)

Is this not the God who armed me well,
Then aimed me in the right direction? (**2 Sam 22:33**)
You touch me and I feel ten feet tall,
You protect me with armor—salvation. (**2 Sam 22:34**)

You have armed me with strength for the battle,
You have subdued my enemies under my feet,
You made them turn and run;
I have destroyed all who hated me. (**2 Sam 22:40-41**)

They called for help,
But no one came to rescue them.
They cried to the Lord,
But He refused to answer them. (**2 Sam 22:42**)

You gave me victory over my accusers.
You preserved me as the ruler. (**2 Sam 22:44**)
Foreigners submit to me,
As soon as they hear, they obey me. (**2 Sam 22:45**)

Live, God! Blessing to my Rock,
My towering Salvation—God!
This God set things right for me,
And shut up the people who talked back. (**2 Sam 22:47**)

He rescued me from enemy anger,
You pulled me from the grip of upstarts,
You saved me from the bullies,
That's why I'm thanking You God. (**2 Sam 22:48**)

Thanking you all over the world,
That's why I'm singing songs,
That rhyme your name and speak Your word.
You give great victories to your king,
Showing unfailing love and mercy to your anointed offspring. (**2 Sam 22:50-51**)

So, I sit here reading Your Word,
Speak into my life,
Reminding me, I'm Your girl,
The One You chose,
To write words of truth,
In books yet unheard—
To the world.

178. My Heart Is Yours

October 8, 2016

I honestly wish my heart were different,
I see the sin within,
It constantly comes to the surface,
And wrecks me over and over again.

Oh Lord my God,
Why do You love me?
Why do You never leave?
Why do You keep forgiving me?
When you know how I can be.

The grace in Your eyes,
Holding me close.

So tender and gentle,
Calling me to repent of my bad choice.
Hits my heart deep within,
And wrecks me over and over again.

My anger, my lack of forgiveness,
My struggle with trust.
Is surrendered to You, Lord,
Whom I absolutely trust.

It's your love for my life,
Your care for my reputation.
You don't just leave me to suffer,
You deal with every specific situation.

Thank You Lord,
For not giving up on me.
Your constant pursuit,
Has wrecked the sin within me.

My heart is Yours,
Here it is.
I love You Lord,
This is what is deep within.

179. My Heart In The Moment

October 8, 2016

My heart in the moment,
Raw and unfiltered,
Exposed because of their tradition,
Not protected but killed.

My God, oh my God,
You see everything.
You know me.
My heart belongs to Thee,
And only to Thee.

My heart belongs to Thee
And only to Thee.
Please guard my heart, King.
For all of eternity,
From the enemy,
Who wants to destroy me.

My heart belongs to Thee,
And only to Thee.
Please restore my heart, King,
Back to the beautiful girl You created in me.

Thank You for loving me.
For redeeming me in the face of those watching.
My heart belongs to Thee,
And only to Thee.
Thank You, King, for delivering me.

180. To Love A Husband

October 8, 2016

Oh, to be able to love a husband,
Like I see some women love their men.
My heart breaks as I see their struggle,
But I so admire them.

So many are selfless,
As they set aside things in life,
Dropping everything,
To remain by their sick husband's side.

I pray for those hurting,
I can't imagine my husband being sick,
Dear Lord Jesus would You heal them,
Draw them close to You,
Hearing their heart's cry from deep within.

I love their example,
One I set aside in my own heart.
One day God will bless me with a husband,
And I'm going to remember the examples I've seen thus far.

181. Does Your Church Love You?

October 9, 2016

Does Your church love You,
Like You long for them to?
Or has Your heart been hurt,
Broken in two?

Forgive us,
For our callous hearts,
Thank You King,
For a new start.

When many left You,
You looked at your disciples that stayed,
Asking the question, "Do you also want to go away?" (**John 6:67**)

But Simon Peter looked at you and said,
"Lord, to whom would we go?" (**John 6:68**)
That thought is ringing in my head.

Where would I go?
This is all I've known,
From the time I was a kid.

182. *Loyal*

October 9, 2016

This question was asked:
"Why are you so loyal to people,
Who are not loyal back?"

As my brother looked me in the eye,
I wondered about my reply.

A loyal person,
Has to be a forgiving person,
In order to remain a loyal person.

183. *Clean Hands*

October 11, 2016

"The righteous keep moving forward,
And those with clean hands,
Become stronger and stronger." (**Job 17:9**)

It's the power of God's Word,
That holds a heart steady,
When a person is facing trials,
Trying to walk righteously.

We never know,
What we will face.
Jesus Christ alone,
Knows the details of our race.

The trial you face,
May be different than mine.
It's not so much the trial that matters,
But how we handled the trials in our life.

God is so good,
He whispers to our heart,
The moment that trial pierces,
Our very heart.

Promises so sweet,
Calling us to cling to His Word,
To not retreat,
But to actively use our sword.

He speaks into our situation,
Knowing we need His direction.
Meeting us right where we are at,
Calling us to obey Him,
While talking to others with tact.

You don't get a choice,
As to the trials you face,
But you do get to choose,
How you handle those trials in this race.

If you have clean hands,
God will make it known.
No one can argue with integrity,
When God is the One who defends His own.

If you have clean hands,
You will only get stronger,
But if you are harboring sin,
Your voice won't have impact any longer.

If you are doing what God has called you to do,
He will carry your voice to the few,
That He wants reached.
So, trust His heart and keep your eyes on your King.

It may not happen today,
But God has His ways.
When you surrender to Him,
His voice reaches the men and women.

184. *God Is The One Who Defended Me*

October 11, 2016

Moments when I sit and think,
"I didn't do this,
God is the One who defended me."

I never said a word.
I prayed and read God's Word.
Pouring out my heart to God,
Praying and praying and praying,
For this storm to stop.

Years ago, I read Hudson Taylor's story.
He said to grow himself in faith,
He would pray and not say anything,
Waiting for God to move and show His glory.

So, I tried it.
It doesn't happen overnight.
However, I truly do believe some prayers,
Were answered immediately in sight.

Moments when I just knew,
The prayer of faith I prayed,
Was answered on cue.
God grew me in faith,
As I followed faithful shoes,
All glory and honor is due.

You, Lord, called me to just pray,
And so I did,
Wanting to simply obey.

I have to obey,
You everyday.

It is difficult,
When something remains.
The heaviness is weighty,
You feel the constant strain.

And then that moment,
The weight is gone.
And a lightbulb goes on.
God defends His own.

There is a time to speak, (**Ecclesiastes 3:7b**)
And a time to stay silent.
God knows what you need,
His message for you is—obedience.

185. *Thankful for my Father and Brothers*

October 11, 2016

I am so thankful,
For my Father, and my brothers.
Humble men,
Loving and sharing Jesus with others.

Shining the light of Jesus Christ,
Where God has placed them in this life.
Loving their family,
Using their gifts for God's glory.

Being the single girl,
In the family,
They always help me,
And just pour on the generosity.
I'm spoiled.
And I know it.
And I'm thankful for it.

No other example do I love,
Than the men in my family,
Making sure I'm taken care of!

They know I'm a Jesus freak,
Going where God calls me,
Being a work missionary.

So, my prayer for them today,
Is that God would shine His face on them,
And bless them,
For being humble men.

186. Thankful for my Mom and Sisters

October 11, 2016

I am so thankful,
For my Mom and sisters,
The Lord truly blessed me with them.
My mom is the giver.
She always seems to show up with something.

How she knows exactly what I need?
Is that a gift?
Or a mom thing?

My mom has never met,
Someone who didn't then become her friend.
She can talk to anyone, it's a gift,
Something many only wish.

"A stranger is just a friend,
You haven't met yet."
My mom always says.
This has been the life lesson,
For all of us kids.

My brothers have it down.
They talk to anyone.
It's their smile that draws the crowd.
My sister-in-laws tell everyone.

My sister is a giver too,
Love her so much.
She understands what I've been going through,
She understands that sometimes finances can be rough.

My sister-in-laws are awesome,
So gifted in different ways.
They are creative, and hardworking,
I love how they have raised their kids.

Family is a blessing,
A sweet gift from God.
Something I am so thankful for,
They are my most favorite people in the world.

187. *Shining Bright*

October 15, 2016

I have been crucified with Christ, (**Galatians 2:20**)
It is no longer I who live,
But Christ.

He lives in me,
And so, this life I live in the flesh,
I live by faith,
In the Son of God.
My Savior, my Redeemer, My Love.

Oh, for grace to live this word.
Every day, going into all the world.
Shining bright as the light,
So women and men see Jesus Christ.

188. *God Chooses*

October 15, 2016

There may be something on your heart that is good,
But this word may be for someone else,
God chooses who,
So, listen for whom He wants to tell.

Love it when God confirms to my own heart,
I pray and pray.
And wait.
Forever. And. A. Day.

Until He whispers to my heart,
And I feel his nudge,
Calling me to write His heart.

And then I wait some more,
Because my timing just doesn't seem to fit His,
And well,
Where in the world is that open door?

I guess I'm learning patience.
My Grandma Grace said she was learning this,
Well into her 90's.
Lord Jesus, seriously,
Will I finally get this down in eternity?

Or maybe,
I'm just not seeing it.
I may walk right past,
The one who should own it.

Or they walked past me?
I'm just saying,
All I know is,
This life sure is interesting.

189. The Holy Spirit's Leading

October 15, 2016

The most exciting times in life,
Are when we follow the Holy Spirit's leading.
Taking steps of faith,
Not clearly seeing.

190. *A New Heart*

October 16, 2016

I want a new heart.
I want new eyes.
I want to see what You see.
I want my heart to break for all those suffering.

Those rejected,
Yet gifted.
Those not chosen,
Because they're not the popular one.

Yet filled with the Holy Spirit,
Ready to reach the lost in the world.
Lord Jesus would You meet them,
And show them the impact of one?

Would You restore a name?
One filled with shame,
Because the gossip that came.
A heart shaking,
Always wondering,
Will this ever change?

I want a new heart,
I want new eyes.
I want to love others like You, Jesus,
For relentless love overcomes fights.

In battle,
Would I pray?
For all those who need to see You today.

We need You,
It's so true.
Lord Jesus would You show us Your glory?
So we can take our eyes off ourselves, and give honor where honor is due.

191. Miracles

October 19, 2016

Miracles in life,
Showcase God's glory,
A sweet reminder that God—
Cares about the quality of your life and your story.

As you walk here on earth,
He meets you right where you are.
He knows what you need,
He loves your heart.

He doesn't want you,
Barely making it in life,
Always struggling,
Feeling the constant strife.

Trials will come,
Storms will arise.
God will meet you,
He will call you to rise.

Rise to recover.
Stand up and walk.
Pour oil into this jar. (**2 Kings 4:1-7**)
Sit down and let's talk.

Constant communion with the Father,
Will heal your heart.
The miracle you are looking for,
Begins when you know His heart.

The heart of a Father,
Who cares for His daughter and son.
Who sees what is up ahead,
El Roi knows what is Best.

Jehovah Raapha—the God who heals.
He can heal you today,
He can meet your need as you kneel.

Jehovah Jireh—the God who provides.
Are you struggling to make ends meet,
Will you come to Him and ask Him why?

It's knowing the heart of your Father,
In your specific situation.
He doesn't have to tell you why,
But come to Him!

For healing takes place
In God's presence.
He is very present,
In your current situation.

Seek His heart.
He loves you so much,
He doesn't want to leave you where you are!

Miracles happen,
When you open the door,
And let God step in. (**Revelation 3:20**)

Miracles in life,
Showcase God's glory,
A sweet reminder that God—
Cares about the quality of your life and your story.

His story for you,
Is better than you can even imagine. (**Ephesians 3:20**)
Come to Him,
And the story will begin.

192. Obedience

October 20, 2016

Obedience to God's voice brings blessing. (**2 Kings 5:10-14**)
It's surrendering to the King.
It releases unnecessary burdens,
He told you to obey for a reason.

It may be something small,
That small step of faith.
Don't rate the size of the step,
Just take that step today.

As you obey,
God will encourage your faith.
And as you obey day by day,
Those steps will increase paving the way.

One day you will look back,
And say, "How did I get here?"

You will see those steps in history,
And those steps of faith once blurry will become clear.

God knows where He wants you,
But He calls you to walk by faith.
Trust Him when you don't see,
For His eyes see clearer than yours on any given day.

193. The Word

October 20, 2016

The Word—
Is God breathed.
By the power of the Holy Spirit,
He speaks to me. (**2 Timothy 3:16-17**)

I need Him so much,
His whispered words in my ear,
I covet.

Opening His Word,
I read.
Praying and listening.
Thankful for His love.
And the direct revelation from above.

A sweet gift,
From God on High.
He loves with words,
As clear as a message written across the sky.

He speaks to me,
All of the time.
I open His Word and read,
"You are Mine." (**Isaiah 43:1**)

The comfort it brings,
Knowing Jesus, my King,
Claims me,
Alleviates any type of fear or suffering.

Thank You King,
For loving me!
You took my place and died on the cross,
Freeing me from the insurmountable cost.

194. Go to Bed

October 20, 2016

Go to bed,
And sleep.
Rest your head.
Don't worry.
God will be,
With you while you sleep.
And He'll join you,
Bright and early.

195. A Gift

October 29, 2016

Those moments of depression,
My eyes are focused on myself.
But the moment freedom steps in,
Is when I proactively reach out to someone else.

It's difficult when all I can see,
Is me.
But the moment my eyes see another hurting,
In need.
I'm free.

It's a need to be needed.
To get my eyes off of me.
I don't want to always think about me,
I want to be free.

When I sit in God's presence,
The depression leaves,
For my eyes are taken off of myself,
And placed on eternity.

The fullness of joy,
Is experienced in God's presence. (**Psalm 16:11**)
It's the opposite of depression.
So, if you are struggling with depression,
Enter God's presence.

When you proactively reach out to others,
Or sit in the presence of the Lord,
You take your eyes off of yourself,
And place them on others or the Lord.

Being consumed with one's issues,
Isolates a mind.
You need to step out the door,
Refresh your mind.

Find someone in need,
And get on your knees.
Start praying for them,
And watch your depression leave.

Miracles happen,
When you help someone else,
It's a miracle in your own life,
A gift of taking your eyes off of yourself.

196. Called to Liberty—Galatians 5:13

October 30, 2016

Abba!
Your divine intervention,
Is needed right now in this nation.
Your presence is what we ask,
Holy Spirit show us our task.
As we are Your hands and feet,
We are the divine intervention this nation needs.

We are appointed,
Anointed,
Ready.
The gifts and call of God cannot be revoked, (**Romans 11:29**)
Nothing can shake us for we are walking steady.

Filled with Your Spirit,
Using our gifts to reach with light,
Those who need to know,
Freedom is found in Jesus Christ,
And we've been called to liberty in this life. (**Galatians 5:13**)

Forgive us for not loving You,
Like You want us to.
For our love is shown,
When we make You known.

Not ashamed,
But fearless.
Impacting all those
In our sphere of influence.

Love speaks,
It is not silent.
For communication frees,
Those walking in darkness.

Abba!
You know who needs to hear,
About Your true loving care.
Please reach their heart,
Comfort those who have missed the mark.
Use us in the world,
To shine the light for that one pearl.

197. "The End"

November 4, 2016

Jesus is returning.
He is so near.
Look around you, friend,
The signs of the times are so clear.

There will be a day,
When ever knee will bow.
Jesus will come with a trumpet shout, (**1 Thessalonians 4:16**)
He will return with the clouds. (**Revelation 1:7**)

It will be so quick,
A twinkling of the eye.
You won't have time to think,
You won't have time to say good-bye.

Are you going to be that one,
Walking around under the sun,
Proclaiming to be a Christian,
But denying the power given from the One above? (**2 Timothy 3:5**)

Having an outward form of godliness, (**2 Timothy 3:5**)
Will not protect you from the end,
If your heart is far from God,
You, my friend, need to repent and be forgiven.

We don't have time to waste.
What you are doing right now,
Is it worth the time to wait,
Should you get on your knees and bow?

There are so many,
Walking this earth,
The person on your right or the person on your left,
May need to hear Jesus' words.

Will you pray to be filled with the Holy Spirit,
Igniting the hearts all around?
Or will you deny the free gift given,
Thinking you can do this on your own?

Here's a question,
One many need to think about—
Are you willing to endure persecution,
Simply so men are reconciled to God?

We are living in the last days,
So many hearts are hardened to the Lord.
They may need to see a hypocrite like you,
To recognize one's worth is found solely in the Lord.

Perfection will not save,
Good works are not good enough.
The only way to heaven,
Is through a relationship with the Lord.

Some run from the heat,
While others run in to save.
What characterizes you right now,
As we are living in the last days?

People like to come up with their own rules,
They change them as they go along.
No one can follow them,
They have no idea what they want.

No person beside Jesus Christ,
Will get you into heaven.
You need to know Him in this life,
Before He says, "The End."

198. Blessed

November 4, 2016

I am blessed,
To listen,
To the whisper of God's heart.
I will keep sitting here,
Talking to the One who created my heart.

I am blessed,
To be a witness.
A light reflecting the Son,
Jesus Christ, the Man who won.

199. The Time is Near—2 Peter 3:9, Revelation 1:3

November 4, 2016

Time.
He's waiting for you.
Time.
He has the best view.

He's watching and waiting,
Though the time is near.
He's moving His children all around,
So that you will hear.

The story of God redeeming mankind,
Rescuing sinners from death.
He's delaying His time,
Waiting for you to repent.

He's waiting for you.
You specifically.
He knows your heart,
He's just waiting for you to start.

Talking to Him,
Like a long lost Friend.
Repenting of sin,
Knowing you are forgiven.

The delay may be longer,
Than some would hope.
Some may mock,
Questioning whether He'll really come.

He's coming.
Just wait.
He's waiting for you.
He's never late.

Time.
Belongs to Him.
He owns it,
He wants you to know you're forgiven.

But you have to come to Him,
And first repent of your sin.
Recognizing you need a Savior,
And your sin separates you from Him.

Time.
He's waiting for you.
Time.
He has the best view.

There is an end,
So, don't wait too long, friend.
Repent of your sin,
Knowing you're forgiven.

200. Conforming To A Law

November 5, 2016

Conforming to a law,
Will not change a heart.
It only leads to a bitter heart,
Just look around you at those who are.

Those who long for freedom,
Feeling restricted by chains.
The chains of bondage,
By one who seeks control over everything.

Control pushes people away,
Knowing they will never measure up,
To the man-made laws of this day and age.

Conforming to a law,
Will not change a heart.
It's an outward action,
Devoid of any heart.

But just like the New Covenant,
Affects the heart.
Jesus came to save,
He is the One that changes our heart.

For anything,
It's a matter of the heart.
Praise God for Christ the Son,
Who regenerates our heart.

201. Writing In My Bible

November 5, 2016

Abba!
As I sit here writing in my bible,
The whispered words You shared with me.
Longing to give this gift to the one whose joy bucket is full,
The one who absolutely loves me.

I have nothing to offer,
But my heart.
To the man You've chosen,
The man that is set apart.

Joy comes from Your Presence, (**Psalm 16:11**)
It's where we are most complete.

Only the man who loves You,
Will love this gift from me.

So many, Abba,
Just read and take.
They don't care about a heart,
They don't care what's at stake.

"Guard your heart,
For it affects everything that you do." (**Proverbs 4:23**)
Your words so clearly stated,
That is what I am trying to do.

The words for my future husband,
To me are so dear,
They are whispered words from You, Abba,
To my heart for only him to hear.

People covet,
What doesn't belong to them.
When they have already received a gift from You,
A husband or wife that You chose for them.

Why take from my husband,
When You already gave them a gift.
That is full of greed and really mean.
When they already have everything they need.

There are seasons in life,
All allowed by Jesus Christ,
Many seasons in the grace of life,
What I look forward to most,
Is sharing them with him as his wife.

Sharing your life,
With the man chosen by Christ,

Best gift ever,
One I've been praying for, for forever.

And. A. Day.
Really, it's been the grace of God
Holding my heart at bay.
But I look forward to the day.

When I get to walk by his side,
Doing what God has called us to do together,
I just long to be with him and abide,
With God, doing whatever.

If my man is not with me,
I don't want anything to do with it.
Conviction on my heart,
I'm standing strong on it.

I am pretty laid back,
But some things I'm firm on.
Being with my man,
And my heart meant only for my husband and God.

I've waited too long,
To be far from him.
I'm called to share my life,
With him, family and friends.

I know the cost is great,
To following You.
But I will follow You Lord,
Wherever You want me to.

202. Be The Change

November 5, 2016

We Christians do not,
Have to accept the way the world is going.
We are here at this time right now,
To be the change.

We do not have to lose our identity,
While the world tries to conform us to its identity.
We were not made in the image of the culture,
For we were created in Christ's image, reflecting His nature.

The world wearies,
While Christ carries.
It's the joy of the Lord,
That makes us want more.

For those that are repentant,
Forgiven and accepted.
But those that walk without conviction,
Forgiven by us yet not trusted.

But if you don't repent to the Lord,
You remain unforgiven.
That's the only thing that matters in this life,
How you are doing with Him?

We want salvation,
Without repentance.
We want a good life,
Without submission to Him.

But you miss it,
When you live for yourself.
You miss the entire meaning of life,
When you refuse to acknowledge Christ above yourself.

People need to see,
Jesus Christ in action.
He moves through you and me,
When we reach out with godly affection.

People need others to be friendly,
So many are so sad and down hearted.
One hug or word you share,
Just might make them laugh and feel accepted.

203. God, Please Strengthen Me

November 5, 2016

God, please strengthen me.
Open my eyes so that I see,
Open my ears so that I hear,
Make me sensitive,
Knowing You are always near.

Illuminate Your heart,
So, my heart doesn't fear.
I trust Your heart, Lord,
You communicate so clear.

I am blessed,
To witness Your glory shine forth,

If only people experienced,
What they were truly created for.

If only they wanted to know,
Your heart even more,
Sitting before You,
Not tired or bored,
Simply wanting more,
Experiencing complete joy.

You love equally,
You have no favorites.
You've designed their life,
To fit them so perfect.

My prayer tonight,
Is that more would simply love You,
Wanting to know Your heart,
Knowing You love them too.

204. Are You Honoring The Lord?

November 8, 2016

Are you honoring the Lord,
Or do you have a love for shame even more? (**Hosea 4:18 NLT**)
Where is your heart,
Is it standing strong or a swinging door?

On one side of the door is honor,
The other side is shame.
You step into either side,
Depending on your mood for the day.

The Lord has given His word,
To protect you from the repercussions of shame,
He loves you so much,
If only you loved Him the same.

Sin is pleasurable for a season
And then comes death.
It's a spiritual death,
That separates you from the One who loved you to death.

Every day you are given an opportunity,
To love honor or to love shame,
A gift of choice God gives to you and me.
Choose to honor God and the demons will flee.

205. Love This Nation

November 8, 2016

I love this nation,
The land of the free.
Thank You Abba for this liberty.
To sit before You praying.

When a nation restricts one's ability to know God,
They play a dangerous game,
A game filled with pain,
A game of momentary fame,
A game remembered with shame,
A game where the nation's name,
Is removed from the list,
Due to its bad decision and death's kiss.

Oh Abba, my prayer today,
Is that You would preserve the church in this nation,
So, the nation experiences a revival and stays,
Strong until the end,
Powerful on up until the day,
Jesus returns and takes His Bride home to stay.

206. A Protected Bride

November 9, 2016

A protected Bride,
So, needed right now.
Lord, thank You for moving,
Thank You for hearing us as we bow.

You are protecting Your church,
With the new President now,
Lord, thank You for moving,
Thank You for hearing us as we bow.

207. Relentless Prayer

November 12, 2016

Relentless prayer,
Is my heart.
I'm not giving up on praying for you,
Wherever you are.

The unconditional love,
God is teaching me,
Is to pray relentlessly,
And watch the demons flee.

Relentless prayer,
Is difficult,
It's spiritual war,
Where the enemy wants you to fold.

So my stubborn heart says, "No."
I'll pray for you,
Wherever you go.

It would be a sin if I didn't pray, (**1 Samuel 12:23**)
Knowing God said, "Don't delay,"
He has a timing for His prayers each day,
Best to listen to Him, and just pray.

You don't need eloquent words,
Often times I've noticed, my simple prayers,
Were the ones that He heard.

So, as I abide with Him, (**John 15:4**)
I pray for all of my fellow brethren,
Trying to be sensitive to His whisper,
Knowing I need to remain current.

Current with Him,
Ready and prepared to battle,
Noticing my heart's burdens,
Are a message He wants to tell.

Wherever you are, how do you correct,
The error of one's thinking?

You repeat the exact words of Christ,
So, they know what He was thinking. (**John 21:23-24**)

People need to hear Christ's heart,
They do not know Him,
So be the one to introduce, wherever you are,
Trusting God to do what you find hard.

Knowing when God's hand is with you,
No one can stop you.
Many will believe and turn,
To the One who was nailed to the tree so that they can learn. (**Acts 11:21**)

Of God's true love,
Experienced in His presence,
Fearless and assured of His glad welcome, (**Ephesians 3:12**)
Witnessing His smile, His true essence.

Don't worry, a pure tool,
God will use. (**2 Timothy 2:21 NLT**)
To get that message,
To the few.

So, don't stop.
Desire an even closer walk with God.
He loves you so much and is so proud,
He sees where you are no matter the crowd,
And He is using you mightily to impact while you first bow,
So, keep training in the shadows,
And He will make your work loud,
Reaching the ones He chose,
Because He loves them and absolutely knows,
They needed to see,
Jesus Christ enter the picture,
And the demons flee.

The spiritual warfare is great,
But God has given you strength,
To overcome the hate,
So, don't stop and remember the inner strength, (**Ephesians 3:16 NLT**)
He's given you to love them and not react in hate.

Yes, I'm praying for you today,
To be filled with His Holy Spirit (**Ephesians 5:18**),
So that you are able to handle whatever comes your way,
Knowing Christ is with you and will say what you can't say.

Relentless prayer,
Is my heart.
I will patiently, persevere in prayer, (**Isaiah 40:31**)
Knowing God will strengthen you wherever you are.

Trusting God's heart,
And His promise to meet you,
Right where you are,
With a word or a bear hug, wrapped in His strong arms,
Safe and secure from the world's harm.

208. *God Is So Faithful*

November 12, 2016

God is so faithful,
He knows right where you are at.
He knows where He wants to grow you,
Would You simply submit to Him?

God will speak to your heart,
And whisper His heart,
"Will you step it up for Me,
I want you to do this so that others will see,"

"Jesus Christ in the flesh,
Loving the world,
With the truth found in His text.
So that they will know
Truth will always flow,
So seamlessly to meet a need,
At the right time to reach someone specifically."

209. Enjoy Your Life

November 12, 2016

People are in different seasons,
In life.
Don't compare,
But enjoy your life right now with Christ.

Prepare now,
For what's to come.
But enjoy your life now,
Thankful for what Christ has done.

Don't always look to tomorrow,
Keep your eyes on today,
For you just might miss that moment,
That will minister to your heart better than any other way.

Don't watch your friends,
Struggling as you compare,
But recognize God has you where,
He wants you because it's best for you there.

When you watch God bless your friends,
While He seems to have forgotten that you yourself are struggling,
Remember, He hasn't forgotten you,
Rejoice with them and change your mood.

God will bless you so perfectly,
It will fit your need so well,
Enjoy how He's moving in your life right now,
Knowing life can change in a minute just like the ringing of a bell.

People are in different seasons,
They are exactly where God wants them.
Recognize there are different needs in different seasons,
And learn contentment as God teaches you about your need in your
current season.

You have a need,
But notice how God is everything you need.
Truly look and see,
Jesus Christ on the tree,
Taking the hit for you and me,
So that we can run through life in every season, free.

210. *Time To Seek The Lord*

November 13, 2016
Plant the good seeds of righteousness,
And you will harvest a crop of love.
Plow up the hard ground of your hearts,
For now it is the time to seek the Lord. (**Hosea 10:12 NLT**)

Your heart has grown so hard,
Due to various experiences in life,
Do you hear God's heart today,
Saying, "Break that hard heart and seek Christ."

Like the soil of the earth,
It gets compacted and pressed in.
Hardened from all those feet,
Walking over its delicate trim.

It's difficult when people,
Don't care about what you do,
And they take what belonged only to you,
Thinking you would feel honored if they did this to you.

When you could care less,
Your heart was more important to you,
Than trying to impress,
Those that don't even know you.

They can live their life,
You were content with your own,
But now your heart has grown hard,
Due to what they have sown.

When someone makes a mistake,
And you reap the consequence,

When someone fails,
And you feel the repercussions of their sin,
How do you deal,
When it hurts you deep within?

You can't control other people,
You can't control what God allows in your life,
But you can control your reactions,
And your attitude that affects your life.

It is time to seek the Lord,
Bring your hard heart to Him,
He is the skilled surgeon,
Who knows how to make it soft once again.
Plant seeds of righteousness,
Wanting the best for someone else,
In turn you will harvest a crop of love,
So much so others will tell.

And the truth of Christ will reach all those who are headed to hell,
Needing to repent of their sin,
Changing their direction,
Running toward heaven,
Reaching all the men and women,
With truth and love,
And all the hard hearts in the world,
Will be broken by the One who loves them from above.

The moment your hard heart breaks,
God reaches those that need their own heart to break.
Maybe God will use you and me,
To reach those who truly needed to see,
The gift of love is found in a soft heart,
Saved and protected, not trampled or critiqued like art.

The love of God softens your heart,
As you truly see,
He loves you just the way you are.
But He wants to transform your heart,
To make you more like Christ,
Not like another woman or man,
So, don't copy them, seek Him.

211. If God Tells Me

November 13, 2016

I will sit,
If God tells me to sit,
I will stand,
If God tells me stand.

I won't surrender to man,
But to God,
Who holds my heart in His hand.

212. A Life Of Repentance

November 13, 2016

What has happened in your life,
Your experiences,
The pain, the strife?

History will only repeat itself,
If you do not lead a life of repentance.
What you experienced in the past,
Will simply show up wrapped in a different present.

213. Abide

November 14, 2016

As you abide, (**John 15:4**)
Christ speaks into your life.

Be fearless as you proclaim,
Jesus Christ's name,
Knowing people are watching you,
To see whether your witness matches your gospel shoes. (**Ephesians 6:15**)

Be fearless in your purity,
No matter the cost.
Stand strong in your convictions,
Knowing God's divine standard of holiness protects you from loss. (**1 Peter 1:16**)

Be fearless in your prayers,
Knowing God cares.
Do not be afraid to come to Him, (**Ephesians 3:12**)
As He personally bends down to listen to what's within, (**Psalm 116:1-2**)
As you bear your sinner heart,
Or your bold prayers that match His heart.

As you abide,
Christ speaks into your life.

His heart,
Becomes your heart.
His desires,
Become your desires.

Everything in life,
Molds you a little more like Christ.
As you take your eyes off of the people or situation,
And focus on Christ and His mission.
You see what Jesus sees,
So many people struggling and in need.
The scars they wear,
Need people to care.
And if Christ has opened your eyes to the need,
He's giving you the opportunity,
To first reach,
Those struggling,

Do you hear Him calling out, "Who will go?"
Will you say, "Yes" or "No."
Christ does not force you,
To do what you do not want to do.
But He has placed a passion on your heart,
For the specific need that matches His heart.

As you abide,
Christ speaks into your life.
He's called you,
Anointed you,
Gifted you.

What are you passionate about?
What is the burden on your heart all about?

That is what He is calling you to do,
So be fearless,

And stand strong in the gift He has given you.
Reaching the many or few,
With Jesus Christ's name,
That adorns you.

214. Focus

November 14, 2016

Focus.
Eyes on Jesus.
Don't worry.
He's with you as you face this.

Whether you are sitting or standing,
Unable to control the hit that is coming.
He's with you as you face this.
Don't worry.
Focus.
Eyes on Jesus.

You cannot control other people.
But Jesus can.
Focus on Him,
And you can face anything.

As your sin temptation surfaces,
As you face those who provoked this,
Don't worry.
Focus.
Eyes on Jesus.

In that moment you will recognize,
Christ is so supreme in your life,
Those facing you, no matter their position or size,
Look so small,
As Jesus Christ reigns, overall.

Whether you have an audience,
Or you are alone,
Remember, Jesus Christ is the cornerstone.

Jesus Christ endured,
More than you ever will.
He set the example for you to follow,
Focus on Him, be still.

Focus.
Eyes on Jesus.
Don't worry.
He's with you as you face this.

215. What Do You See?

November 14, 2016

When you look out,
What do you see?
Is the water choppy?
Or glassy?

Does that decide,
Whether you will throw your foot over the side,

Of the boat you are in,
As you look out and see someone struggling?

Glassy water,
Means it's smooth sailing for you.
What they are struggling with is easy,
You can help them and it not be a sacrifice to you.

But choppy water,
Now that's another story.
Even while rowing in the boat, the headwind,
Felt like you were pulling a deadman underwater.

The strain it caused,
Made you heave and pause,
If you helped now,
The sacrifice might be too much for you to count.

What's the whisper in your ear?
As Jesus calls you to obey.
Will you look back on this time and be ashamed,
You looked the other way?

216. Resisting

November 14, 2016

If one person is resisting the Lord,
Everyone on the boat will feel the storm. (**Jonah 1:4-16**)

Are you praying as intensely,
As you were before?

That name just seemed to pop to your mind,
And you were immediately interceding until you saw the answer.
Or has your desire decreased?
You got annoyed, -
The spiritual warfare had increased.

Are you serving the Lord,
Like you once did.
Or has your focus diminished?

Are you using your gifts,
Right where God has placed you?
Or are your eyes searching,
Wanting to be someplace new?

You are on a boat,
With a team around you.
Are you resisting the Lord right now?
Just look,
You'll know,
If your team is going down.

Are prayers being answered?
Are they excelling?
Or are they all struggling,
Because you have been resisting?

God's mercies are new every day,
What's the burden on your heart today?
Look at your team,
What do you see?

217. Ephesians 3:12

November 15, 2016

Repent of your sin,
And fearlessly enter in.
To the presence of Your Lord,
Assured,
That He welcomes you, forgiving your sin.
Loving you,
With His face shining through and through.

218. Remember The Good

November 16, 2016

Remember the good,
When your heart starts remembering the trials,
That brought so much sorrow,
Remember the good.

Purpose in your heart to remember,
How Jesus stood so close.
Don't focus on the past,
But use that history to make the most,
Of today by reaching the struggling,
Who need to know,
Jesus stands close to the hurting,
He never leaves His sheep to go.

219. *Christ Is Close*

November 16, 2016

A pure life,
Sees Christ. (**Matthew 5:8**)
Their safe haven,
Free from the storm coming.
For Christ is close.

That sensitive heart,
Focused on the Lord.
Abiding in His presence,
Wanting to hear His voice even more.

So addicted to His voice,
His soft, calm words that comfort,
So soothing in one's ear,
You simply sit and listen wanting Him near.

Every time He speaks,
He meets your exact need.
And so you write what you hear,
So others know He is near.

For Christ is close!
In more ways than one.
He's standing right next to you,
Never leaving your side for a better view.

He's close.
Do you see Him?
Please repent of your sin,
So your eyes will be opened,

For His return is imminent.
For Christ is close.

220. In Life

November 18, 2016

In life,
We need to make the change,
When God says move,
And we need to pray to be content, (**Philippians 4:11**)
When God tells us to.

221. Struggling With Anger

November 21, 2016

How do you stop,
Struggling with anger?
That issue so pressing,
You constantly remember.

It was wrong,
What you faced.
But how do you stop struggling,
Not wanting to struggle with hate.

Why is your memory so good?
Who knows.

But Satan can be the Great Historian,
Bringing to your remembrance what you wish you didn't know.

Doesn't Jesus forgive the past and forget?
He remembers the good,
But He chooses to forget,
The repentant sin that was not so good.

Choose to be like Christ.
The Best Historian who actually paid the price,
To redeem the wrong,
Saving a life.

A historian studies the past,
To mimic the good,
And change the bad.

When you remember,
Don't grow in anger,
Choose to see,
How you can make the change to free,
All those who are also unnecessarily struggling.

So how do you stop,
Struggling with anger?
You focus on Jesus Christ,
Your Redeemer.

Your Redeemer lives,
He is seated on the throne.
He is interceding for you specifically,
Knowing what they have done.

Your Redeemer seeks to save,
He rescues from harm,

At the perfect time,
He steps in with His strong arm.

Instead of growing in anger,
Purpose in your heart,
To have the eyes to see,
Jesus, your Redeemer, stepping in fearlessly.

222. You Promised

November 21, 2016

You promised,
You would give me shepherds after Your own heart,
To feed me with knowledge and understanding, (**Jeremiah 3:15**)
To guide me in regard to my part.

223. Divine Test

November 22, 2016

The divine test for younger men,
If you don't step in and save a sister in Christ,
Will someone step in and save your wife?

Do unto others as you would want done to you,
God placed you there for a reason,
What's the burden on your heart calling you to do?

224. *Please Smile*

I love Your Word,
Oh God.

Today, please,
Smile your blessing smile (**Psalm 80:3 MSG**)
Cause Your face to shine for miles.
Those sweet answers to prayer,
As You bend down and smile at Your heirs.

225. *Healed*

November 26, 2016

You heal,
In so many ways.
So thankful for Your touch,
That touched my heart today.

I sit before You,
And talk.
A lot.
And I hear Your voice whisper,
"Daughter,
Your faith has made you well,
Go in peace and be healed."

"Go in peace and be healed,"
Is ringing on my heart.

Peace is a gift,
That can only come from You, Lord. (**John 14:26-27**)

Peace with God,
Means everything to me.
It's that assurance on a heart,
That He is pleased with me.

So, I will go in peace,
My faith has made me well.
Many stories to tell,
As I share how Jesus Christ made me well.

His presence in my life,
His voice in my ear,
He never left my side,
His words so clear.

We never know,
What we will face in life,
It's not so much what we face,
But how we handle everything in stride.

Best to remain in God's presence,
For He is always in control.
Just talk to God,
And hear His voice over all.

Don't ever feel guilty for spending time in God's presence,
Those who make you feel that way,
Were never true friends.

Quality time and quantity,
Is what you need,
If you want to experience a touch,
Close to the heart of Your King.

Jesus is returning,
He wants you to know Him before He comes.
Do you know Jesus?
A sensitive heart will say, "Yes! Come Lord Jesus come."

Do you need a touch today?
A spoken word from the Lord,
To heal what is hindering your day?
Then seek Him, keep seeking Him in His word.

226. *Sensitive Heart*

November 26, 2016

Some may wonder,
How a heart can be so sensitive?
I personally believe it comes from spending time with the Lord,
Jesus is the One that makes a person sensitive.

Jesus allows us to go,
As deep as we want to go.
The question really should be,
Do you really want the key?

The key to His heart?
I want that key.
So, I spend as much time as He will let me,
For that is how we come to know,
The One who holds the world.

To know His heart,
We have to spend time with His heart.

His heart is displayed for all to read,
It's the Bible, see?

Sensitivity doesn't just come,
It's a mark of the indwelling presence of God.
He whispers to your heart,
Through His word.
Making you sensitive to what He wants,
Obedience.

Wisdom comes from the Lord,
When you obey the Lord.
Don't expect to be wise,
If you only obey your own made up reasons why.

So many want to hear God's voice,
They want to be sensitive to His leading,
But they don't want to take the time,
To truly get to know the One who is leading.
Or obey the One who sees everything.

Honor is due,
To the One who is on the throne.
Jesus Christ, our Lord,
Savior, Redeemer, and Friend.

Our Rescuer, our Healer,
Our Provider.
El Roi sees everything,
Come sit with Him and see what He is currently viewing.

Do you want to be sensitive?
Do you want to know the reason for those impressions on your heart?
Then sit with Him,
And He will tell you whether those impressions are true or not.

Why am I so sensitive?
I believe it's because I'm called to pray.
There is one specific person on my heart,
The Lord put him on my heart last year, and the name is still there today.

227. I Failed Again

November 27, 2016

I failed again.
The guilt overwhelms me,
It holds me back,
From running free.

Simple obedience,
Is what the Lord asks.
It's just a message,
For someone who shouldn't have to ask.

But my fear holds me back,
Who am I to share?
My eyes quickly look to myself,
And I forget why I am truly here.

I am here to serve God,
However He likes,
Who am I to say no,
I know I am not as wise.

I walked right past,
Yet again.

The guilt hit me,
And I walked back only to recognize, I missed God's timing.

Every time this happens to me.
Why am I not quick to obey?
I seem to always run the other way.

I just need to share it,
That's all.
I could be the one wrong,
God is the One who confirms to all.

It's not like I want to keep it,
I need to give it away.
I just have no clue,
Who this is for today.

God gives us opportunities
To step in.
Why do we look away?
When a quick word is all that is needed.

One word,
Can change someone's day.
I know this from experience,
And my guilt sits wanting to stay.
So, I repent of my lack of obedience,
And seek God again,
Praying He will open,
That door for a second chance to share this word with the men and women.
Trusting that if the word is from God,
It will hit their heart deep within,
And as they take that word to God,
He will confirm or deny it.
But I took that step of faith in obedience,

Trusting that I heard,
God's voice in His Word.

We never know if just one word,
Will impact a heart.
Why Christian, do we hold back,
We don't know what they've been through thus far.
But God knows,
And if He burdened our heart,
He's calling us to obey.
This is obedience not art.

God speaks.
He speaks directly.
And today He wants to use you and me,
To speak directly,
To those struggling,
Needing to be free,
Hearing His voice speak directly,
Impacting a life here and now and on into eternity.

One word,
Can encourage a heart,
Reminding a friend that God says,
"I see you, where you are, (**Hebrews 13:5-6**)
I sent this person because I care personally about your heart, (**1 Peter 5:7**)
I love you, (**John 3:16**)
I am with you, (**Matthew 28:20**)
And I'm proud of what you have done thus far, (**Mark 1:11**)
So keep going and don't stop.
There will be a day when you will see,
All those lives you impacted for eternity. (**Matthew 6:21**)
Trust Me."

228. A Good Friend

November 28, 2016

What is the truth,
God is teaching you?
That is the lesson to learn,
For that is God's test for you,
That is what He wants you to discern.

What God is speaking to your heart today,
Is the lesson He wants you to take in,
He has a lesson for you every day,
You are a student of Him.

Every lesson taught,
Every message given,
Every book written,
Should come from one who abides with Him.

That is one anointed,
Filled with the Holy Spirit,
Because they are submitted to Him,
Obeying His direction using their gifts.

One lesson God has been teaching me,
Is how to be a true friend.
What is a true friend?
One who steps in.

God has given everyone different gifts,
Look at your friends,
Are you gifted differently or do you have the same gift?

Oftentimes I truly believe,
God places people around us that are gifted differently.
An opportunity,
To be a true friend,
And step in,
Using your gift,
To cover your friend's weakness,
Making them look good,
In the face of the world.

Why don't people want to help others look good?
Because people want themselves to look good.
It's not the right Christian attitude,
And they know it,
If they had the right Christian attitude,
They would have just stepped in and no one would have even known it.

That's a true friend,
One who simply steps in.
Using their gift,
To elevate their friend.

They don't need the spotlight,
They are confident in their gift,
Knowing God is pleased,
When they use it.

And that's all that matters,
In this life,
Pleasing Christ.

People who are gifted the same,
Confirm God moving through another.
When will we finely grasp,
Pleasing Christ is all that matters.

I choose to step in,
And be that friend,
Who doesn't need a spotlight,
But knows she is gifted.

I want to please Jesus Christ.
That's all that matters to me in this life.
And so, when He calls me to simply step in,
I will do so because I want to be a good friend.

229. God's Presence

November 28, 2016

God's presence is a reality,
Not just a memory.
He is currently,
Here.
He doesn't come once a year,
You don't have to go through anybody,
Jesus is here.

230. Please Confirm

November 29, 2016

Praying today,
For that word on my heart.
That if it is the Lord's will,

God would confirm it,
But if I'm wrong God would remove it.

God confirms through His Word,
Other people,
And circumstances that align with His Word.

All three tend to fit,
So, Lord Jesus,
Here it is.
Please confirm or correct this impression,
With whomever You wish.

231. Outsider/Insider

November 30, 2016

Outsider.
Insider.
Outside.
In.
Don't we all feel one way or the other,
No matter the place we are in?

232. My prayer—Psalm 9

December 1, 2016

How will the nations know,
They are but men, (**Psalm 9:20b**)
Unless You LORD step in,
And rescue the oppressed and the forsaken?

You alone are a refuge for the oppressed,
A refuge in times of trouble. (**Psalm 9:9**)
And those who know your name trust in You,
For You LORD have never abandoned anyone who searches for You. (**Psalm 9:10**)

You don't forget the cry of the humble,
You don't forget their cry for help.
You avenge their blood and remember them, (**Psalm 9:12**)
Oh sing praises to the LORD, those who dwell in Zion! (**Psalm 9:11**)

The LORD reigns forever,
Executing judgment from His throne. (**Psalm 9:7**)
He will judge the world with justice,
And rule the nations with the fairness for which He is known. (**Psalm 9:8**)

For the needy will not be forgotten forever,
The hopes of the poor will not always be crushed. (**Psalm 9:18**)
Arise, O LORD! Do not let the mortals defy You!
Let the nations be judged. (**Psalm 9:19**)

233. Oh, To Know You

December 1, 2016

Oh, to know You,
Like I want to know You.
To hear Your heart.
Jesus please show me,
Exactly who You are.

The most cherished gift in the grace of life,
Is knowing You as Your bride.
Teach me how to love,
Help me to be humble, elevating others, seeking to unite. (**Philippians 2**)
Lord, I need You,
To speak to me tonight.

234. The Best Gift

December 1, 2016

I pray for my future husband,
All of the time.
If people knew me,
They would know this bible of mine,
Is a gift— one of a kind.
Handwritten notes,
Journaled in the margins,
Prayers for men and women,
Covering,
Whomever the Lord puts on my heart,
As I'm staring down at the page.

I have different names written throughout,
Those the Lord called me to cover that day.
I look forward to meeting this man,
God has set apart for me.
I can't wait to give him my bible,
Because it's a part of me.
My heart intertwined with God's heart,
The best gift I could think of,
To give to the man,
Who will be a gift to me straight from above. (**James 1:17**)

235. My Birthday

December 1, 2016

My birthday is on 9/11.
I turned 18 that day.
I woke up to my sister opening my bedroom door,
Saying, "Happy birthday,"
And, "We got bombed by terrorists today."

I love my country,
That hit deep.
No I don't work for the government,
But my loyalty runs deep.
I sat on the couch the entire day,
Watching the news troubled and dismayed.
Broken for my nation that experienced horrific tragedy that Tuesday,
A darkened day.

Candles were lit,
Everywhere.
Honoring every life that was lost because of terrorists.

The nation was praying,
All of the men and women.
The church was packed Sunday,
As people streamed in to find comfort and a safe haven.

I love praying for this nation,
For the men and women in their different positions.
For the president who leads,
For security and God's peace.
For hearts to surrender to the King of Kings,
Oh, for a nation to remember the Christ centered foundation that brings,
Stability.
In a world suffering.

God is faithful.
He is present in the land.
Oh, for the church to rise up,
And reach out even more to the lost, taking a stand.

Jesus Christ saves,
In God we trust,
Oh, nation please remember,
The One who absolutely loves us.

For God so loved the world,
He gave His only begotten Son,
If you repent of your sin and believe in Jesus Christ,
No matter what happens in this life—you've won.

236. My Family

December 1, 2016

My family is amazing,
I'm so blessed by them.
My nieces and nephews are so loved,
What did we ever do before them?

They love to run and jump into my arms,
The sweetest gift to my single heart.

I love them so much,
I love them like they were my own.
Oh, to have children like them one day,
They make me smile and my face glow.

Children know when they are safe and secure,
You can tell when their joy buckets are full.
They are loved by all,
Pointed to Jesus Christ above all.

237. Words Remain

December 3, 2016

Words remain,
They go over and over through a head,
Leaving a stain.

I'm guilty of misusing my words,
Just like you.

Oh, Lord forgive us,
For not seeing Jesus Christ in the person we purposefully subdued.

Words inflicted by the tongue,
Can only be healed,
With Words from the Stronger One,
Jesus Christ, the Prince of Peace.

Lord Jesus will You speak,
To every heart that needs,
A healing Word,
To overcome the mean-spirited words.

He who guards his mouth,
Preserves his life,
But he who opens wide his lips,
Shall have destruction far and wide. (**Proverbs 13:3**)

Anxiety in the heart of man,
Causes depression,
But a good word makes it glad, (**Proverbs 12:25**)
And he is able to overcome all opposition.

Would we seek to support,
Instead of tearing down those who need our support?
Tell the truth of course,
But there is a tactful way to share a discourse.

Speak truth in love,
Seek to build up,
Not destroy,
Only Jesus could drink the cup,
So why are we making life hard so others cannot enjoy.

Repent and ask for forgiveness,
Knowing you want to be treated with respect, too.

Don't put on others,
What God has called you to do.

238. *Seeing Clearly*

December 3, 2016

Is Jesus in your view?
What are you looking at?
Who is staring back at you?
God cares about the integrity of His house.
Do you?

Blessed are the pure in heart,
For they shall see God. (**Matthew 5:8**)
Today, how is your heart?
Are you seeing clearly what you should?

239. *In A Season*

December 3, 2016

In a season celebrating Christ's birth,
And the reason He came,
To redeem and show people's true worth,
By the power of His name.

240. Songs in the Night

December 3, 2016

Oh, songs in the night,
My heart cries out through you.
With my hand stretched out, (**Psalm 77:2**)
I pray continuously hidden from their view.

I search for the Lord,
All night long I pray.
Hands lifted towards heaven,
Pleading my case.
My spirit overwhelmed,
I cannot sleep.
I continue praying,
Longing for relief.

I think of the good old days, (**Psalm 77:5**)
Long since ended,
When my nights were filled with joyful songs, (**Psalm 77:6**)
And I wonder why now I feel so rejected.

Will the Lord never again show me favor? (**Psalm 77:7**)
Is His unfailing love gone forever? (**Psalm 77:8**)
Has His promises failed forevermore? (**Psalm 77:8**)
Has God forgotten to be kind? (**Psalm 77:9**)
Has He slammed the door on His compassion tonight? (**Psalm 77:9**)

Remembering the times of joy,
Just makes me more depressed. (**Psalm 77:6**)
I search for the solution to the problem,
But find nothing to redeem me from this mess.

As I sit here crying through the night,
I remember that one time.
Your right hand protected me, (**Psalm 77:10**)
It kept me safe and strengthened me at the perfect time.

Purposing now to remember Your wonderful deeds,
Focusing on the fact that You still part Red Seas, (**Psalm 77:16**)
I sit here meditating on all Your work,
Thankful Lord to be called Yours.

Prayers forever prayed,
When answered are miracles displayed,
Testimonies of the tried and true,
Faith strengthened when one prays,
Seeking only God's eternal view.

Oh, songs in the night,
My heart cries out through you.
With my hand stretched out, (**Psalm 77:2**)
I pray continuously seeking God's view.

You are holy, Oh Lord,
Righteous and pure.
You still perform miracles,
You rescue the unheard.

You redeem Your people with Your arm, (**Psalm 77:15**)
Your strength is what keeps everyone from harm.

With a spoken word,
Everything can change,
Oh Lord, please turn my songs in the night,
Into songs of day.

241. *Redemption Day*

December 10, 2016

Days of redemption,
Thank You Lord.
You held my heart,
Calling me Yours.

You owned it,
Like no other.
Thank You Lord,
For the open door. (**Revelation 3:8**)

What does it take?
It takes believing in faith.
Endless thanks,
Oh Lord, for redemption day.

242. *Fit for Eternity*

December 11, 2016

Abba! How do You,
Want me to serve You?

My prayer today as I sit here:
Reading
Wondering
Dreaming
Envisioning
Repenting

Praying
Meditating

I love You Lord,
I know You have given me various gifts.
How do You want me to serve You in the world;
Where do I fit?

Are gifts for different seasons?
Is there a time for everything?
What is the reason,
For this season of suffering?

People are gifted differently,
You can't assume.
I have felt so lost Lord,
Not knowing what to do.

Except,
Pray and write,
And that is what I have been doing every night.

Thank You Lord
For never leaving me,
Assuring me,
Comforting me,
Yes, even correcting me,
Showing me,
Sharing with me,
Molding me,
So, I am fit for eternity.

243. *The Gift Of Shepherding*

December 16, 2016

The gift of shepherding,
Is speaking truth in love.
The shepherd cares, knowing they are entrusted,
With the lives of others from God above.

244. *A Heart With No Voice*

December 17, 2016

My God, my God, (**Psalm 22:1**)
I feel abandoned, forsaken, lost,
This expression on my heart Lord is so strong,
What is the cost?

There is hope,
I believe it,
I will continue to cry out Your name Lord,
Believing You hear me say it.

It's hard to speak,
No words come,
A heart with no voice,
Lord, what have they done?

My heart displayed,
Few words spoken to their face,
Mocked by those who came,
They sneer at me and shake their head with hate.

But You are holy, (**Psalm 22:3**)
The praises of Israel surround You.
Our fathers trusted You, (**Psalm 22:4**)
They trusted and You delivered them from the hateful crew.

They cried to You and were delivered, (**Psalm 22:5**)
They trusted in You and were not ashamed.
My God, my God even though You haven't responded to me,
I know You hear and You know my name - (**Isaiah 43:1**)

You brought me safe from my mother's womb, (**Psalm 22:9 NLT**)
And led me to trust You,
You have been my God from the moment I was born, (**Psalm 22:10 NLT**)
Thank You Lord, for I am Yours.

Be not far from me, (**Psalm 22:11**)
For trouble is near,
There is none to help me,
I know You hear.

Every night You hear my voice, (**Psalm 22:2b NLT**)
But I find no relief.
Yet, I know You hear,
I know You are near.
Please rescue me from this overwhelming fear.

I need You close to me, O God,
You are the only One that can save.
These enemies surrounding me are vicious like dogs, (**Psalm 22:20**)
I am seriously exhausted from their stupid cause.

They look and stare at me. (**Psalm 22:17b**)
But I know You are near me.
You have answered me.
You have rescued me.

Thank You for You have answered me. (**Psalm 22:21b**)
No more silence,
I hear You clearly.

I will declare Your name loudly, (**Psalm 22:22**)
In the midst of everyone I will praise You,
Lord, You are too good.

The poor shall eat and be glad, (**Psalm 22:26a**)
Those who seek You will praise You,
No heart will be sad.

For You have not ignored the suffering of the needy, (**Psalm 22:24 NLT**)
You have not turned or walked away,
You have listened to their cries of help,
You stepped in and made a way.

Let Your heart live forever,
Shining bright in our lives,
God, You deliver,
At the perfect time.

Future generations will serve You, (**Psalm 22:30 NLT**)
Our children will hear about the wonders of the Lord,
Your righteous acts will be told to the unborn, (**Psalm 22:31a NLT**)
Thank You Lord!

245. My Shepherd

December 18, 2016

The Lord is my Shepherd, (**Psalm 23:1 NLT**)
I have everything I need.
He lets me rest in green meadows; (**Psalm 23:2 NLT**)
He leads me beside peaceful streams.

His name is Jehovah-Jireh,
The God who provides.
My Shepherd meets every need I have,
Blessing me even more with gifts from on high.

He says, "Come unto Me all who are weary,
And heavy laden and I will give you rest." (**Matthew 11:28**)
His yoke is easy and His burden is light, (**Matthew 11:30**)
He didn't come to burden us but to alleviate burdens in our life.

That is always the question,
When we are overly weary.
Are we doing what the Lord has asked of us,
Or are we doing something without seeking Him, praying consistently?

The Lord says, "Seek Me and you shall find Me," (**Jeremiah 29:13**)
He will guide me with His eye. (**Psalm 32:8**)
He leads by communicating so clearly, (**Isaiah 30:21**)
I know He remains right by my side. (**Matthew 28:20**)

He renews my strength, (**Psalm 23:3 NLT**)
He guides me along right paths,
Bringing honor to His name.
O Lord, thank You for Your goodness and overwhelming grace.

I know that my Redeemer lives, (**Job 19:25**)
He's seated on the throne,
Interceding and loving me, (**Hebrews 7:25**)
It's by God's grace that I am not alone.

Even when I walk through, (**Psalm 23:4 NKJV**)
The valley of the shadow of death,
I will fear no evil,
For my Shepherd is stronger than them.

You, O Lord, are close beside me, (**Psalm 23:4b NLT**)
Your rod and Your staff,
Protect and comfort me.
Your presence in my life holds me steady,
That is why I do not fear what comes at me.

You prepare a feast for me, (**Psalm 23:5 NLT**)
In the presence of my enemies.
You welcome me as a guest,
Anointing my head with oil in front of all the rest.

My cup overflows with blessings, (**Psalm 23:5b NLT**)
I really have no words to describe,
The incredible blessing that comes,
When Your face shines. (**Psalm 67:1**)

Surely your goodness and unfailing love, (**Psalm 23:6 NLT**)
Will pursue me all the days of my life,
And I will live in the house of the Lord forever,
Waiting for You to return to claim me as Your Bride.

In the meantime, I will be found redeeming the time, (**Ephesians 5:16**)
Praying for You to hurry up and come, (**Revelation 22:20**)
To take me home as Your Bride. (**Revelation 19:7**)

246. The Weeping Prophet

December 20, 2016

Jeremiah, the weeping prophet,
Spoke the heart of God,
To a people whose hearts turned far from God.

"When they ask you why, Jeremiah, (**Jeremiah 16:10-13**)
This is what you are to say:
'You turned your heart away,
Now I'm sending you far away.'"

"Because you have forsaken Me,
And you have not kept My law,
Each one of you only follows,
The dictates of your own evil heart,
Refusing to listen to Me and My heart."

"You chased after other gods,
Worshiping that which cannot save you.
So, I'm sending you to a land you do not know,
Where you will get your fill of worshipping gold statues.
A land where I will not show favor to you."

Has God ever spoken this to your heart,
Calling you out on the idol in your heart?
Maybe it's a warning of what's to come,
If you don't repent of your idol worship,
Worshipping only The One.

The One who came to seek and to save,
Jesus Christ is His name,
The only One worthy,
To dictate a life that reflects His image and name.
Jesus is the One you are to worship,
Do you need to repent today?

Purify your heart,
Repent and be made new.
Jesus is returning,
God loves you.

247. *Perfect Time*

December 22, 2016

As I have struggled tonight,
I am reminded,
A note or a word,
Comes at the perfect time.

God has a timing,
For His words to reach His kids.
I found a note tonight,
That reached my heart through His.

248. A Shepherd's Presence

December 23, 2016

We know the presence of God,
Is so powerful in our lives.
We know He is right by our side.

The presence of a shepherd is powerful, too.
A tool God uses that people can see.
Someone willing to be Jesus' hands and feet.

249. Love You Lord

December 23, 2016

I love You Lord,
So, thankful You came,
Born in a manger,
Dying the death that had my name.

Taking my place,
Freeing me from disgrace.
Covering my shame,
With Your name.

So, thankful for You,
No words will ever truly express,
My heart for You.

So, I will live my life,
Seeking Your heart,

The greatest expression of love,
Living Your heart.

250. Love Divine

December 24, 2016

This one is mine,
Love divine,
Given to me,
From God's gold mine.

His word so profound,
Speaks straight into my heart.
I will cling to this word,
Trusting God and His heart.

I will seek His face,
I will sit and listen,
Knowing God will speak to me,
Trusting His word so clearly spoken.

251. Love For You Held Me:

The Moment God Turned His Back on Jesus
December 24, 2016

A season of silence so difficult,
I'm isolated and alone.

You turned Your head away,
But I'm the only One that knows.

This separation is too much to bear,
They don't even realize,
I need You right here,
I need Your eyes so clear.
Your voice in my ear.
Your presence with Me is what removes all fear.

My God, My God,
Why have You forsaken Me? (**Psalm 22:1**)
I cry in the daytime,
But You do not answer Me.

You hear My voice, (**Psalm 22:2b NLT**)
But I find no relief.
Why have You turned,
Your back on Me?

A season of silence so difficult,
I'm isolated and alone.
Your presence in my life, Lord,
Is all I know.

My life is poured out like water, (**Psalm 22:14a NLT**)
And all my bones are out of joint.
I am but a worm, (**Psalm 22:6a**)
Scorned by men who say, "He trusted in the LORD." (**Psalm22:7-8**)

O LORD, do not stay away! (**Psalm 22:19 NLT**)
For You alone are My strength.
Please come quickly to My aid!
Your presence is what I need right now on this day.

I love You, LORD,
That will never change.
Love for You held Me,
On the cross this dark day.

Your presence in My life,
Brought me joy in the past.
Father into Your hands I commit My Spirit, (**Luke 23:46**)
Breathing My last.

A season of silence so difficult,
I lived for the world.
For the joy that was set before Me, (**Hebrews 12:2**)
I endured the cross, despising the shame for one pearl.

My Father turned His back on Me,
So you could be healed.
The pain so restricting,
The hostility overwhelming,
But love for you held Me.

A promise of eternity in heaven,
Is given to those,
Who repent of their sin,
Seek to be forgiven,
Recognizing they need a Savior,
To take the hit meant for them.

252. "Fail Forward"

December 25, 2016

Whenever I read the book of Proverbs,
My heart is overwhelmed,
By my failure,
At living the words spoken.

But I'm reminded of the cross,
And the reason Jesus came,
To take my guilt away,
Reminding me He forgives my sin over and over again.

Even this morning,
I woke up with guilt.
My own hostility at situations,
Making my own heart sick.

And my failure,
At sharing a simple word.
"You're a failure,"
Kept going through the head of this girl.

Have you ever wondered,
What would have happened,
If you had obeyed,
When God told you to go that way?

What do you do,
When failure overwhelms you?
I purposefully remind myself of the cross,
Remembering the words,
I once heard,
"Fail forward."

Run to the cross,
When your eyes are opened to the cost,
Of your sin,
On men and women.

When your eyes are opened,
To how sinful your heart truly is,
Fall to your knees and repent,
Thanking the Lord Jesus for His grace and forgiveness.

253. Blessed Is He

December 25, 2016

Blessed is he, (**Psalm 32:1**)
Whose transgression is forgiven,
Whose sin is covered,
Whose name is found in heaven.

Blessed is the man, (**Psalm 32:2**)
Whose record the LORD has cleared of sin,
Whose lives are lived,
In complete honesty before all men and women.

When I kept silent, (**Psalm 32:3**)
I was weak and miserable,
Day and night Your hand of discipline was heavy on me, (**Psalm 32:4**)
My strength evaporated and I was unable.

So I acknowledged my sin to You, (**Psalm 32:5**)
My iniquity I have not hidden,

I said, "I will confess my transgressions to the LORD."
And You forgave the iniquity of my sin.

Therefore, let all the godly confess their sin to You, (**Psalm 32:6**)
While there is still time,
That they may not drown in the floodwaters of judgment,
But rescued from that which holds down their life.

For you are my hiding place; (**Psalm 32:7**)
You protect me from trouble,
You surround me with songs of deliverance,
I know God is able.

To do exceedingly, abundantly, (**Ephesians 3:20**)
More than I can even think or ask.
Thank You LORD for forgiving me,
Taking the weight of sin off my back.

The LORD says, "I will guide you along, (**Psalm 32:8**)
The best path for your life,
I will advise you and watch over you,
Guiding you with My eye."

Unfailing love, (**Psalm 32:10**)
Surrounds those who trust the LORD,
Rejoice in the LORD and be glad, (**Psalm 32:11**)
All you who obey Him and whose hearts are pure!

254. *Rejoice Everyone, Rejoice!*

December 26, 2016

Sing to Him a new song; (**Psalm 33:3 NKJV**)
Play skillfully with a shout of joy.
Rejoice!

Rejoice in the LORD, O you righteous! (**Psalm 33:1 NKJV**)
Rejoice in the LORD, everyone.
For praise from the upright is beautiful. (**Psalm 33:1 NKJV**)
Sing and let's praise the name of Christ— the Son.

For the word of the LORD holds true, (**Psalm 33:4 NLT**)
And everything He does is worthy of our trust!
Rejoice in the LORD, everyone,
See what God has done for all of us!

He loves whatever is just and good, (**Psalm 33:5 NLT**)
And His unfailing love fills the earth.
The LORD merely spoke and the heavens were created, (**Psalm 33:6 NLT**)
He breathed the Word—

All the stars were born.
He gave the sea its boundaries, (**Psalm 33:7 NLT**)
And locked the oceans in vast reservoirs.
Rejoice everyone, in the LORD!

Let everyone in the world fear the LORD, (**Psalm 33:8 NLT**)
Let everyone stand in awe of Him,
For when He spoke the world began, (**Psalm 33:9 NLT**)
It appeared at His command.

What joy for the nation whose God is the LORD, (**Psalm 33:12**)
Whose people He has chosen for His own.

The Lord looks down from heaven, (**Psalm 33:13-14**)
He observes the whole human race from His throne.

The Lord made their hearts, (**Psalm 33:15**)
He understands everything they do,
God is the potter, you are the clay,
Do you know what God has called you to do?

The best equipped army cannot save you, (**Psalm 33:16**)
Nor is great strength enough to uphold you,
Don't count on your war horse for victory, (**Psalm 33:17**)
But on the Lord who watches over you with mercy. (**Psalm 33:18**)

Rejoice in the Lord everyone,
For He alone rescues from death, (**Psalm 33:19**)
Keeping people alive in famine,
Saving those with His blood—crimson red.

We depend on the Lord alone,
To save us,
For only He can help us,
Protecting us,
With a shield formed specifically for us.

In Him our hearts rejoice! (**Psalm 33:21**)
Rejoice everyone, rejoice!
We trust in His holy name, (**Psalm 33:21**)
For Love came.

Let Your unfailing love surround us, O Lord, (**Psalm 33:22**)
For our hope is in You alone.
Rejoice everyone in the Lord,
Rejoice!

255. *Don't Worry*

December 30, 2016

Don't worry about the wicked, (**Psalm 37:1**)
Don't envy those who do wrong,
Their time on earth is but a moment,
The ungodly who prosper know where they belong.

For like grass, they soon fade away, (**Psalm 37:2**)
Like springtime flowers they wither,
Trust in the LORD, my friend, and do good, (**Psalm 37:3**)
Then you will live safely in the land and prosper.

Delight yourself also in the LORD, (**Psalm 37:4**)
And He shall give you the desires of your heart.
Simply enjoy God,
And He will place His desires on your heart.

His desires will become your desires,
As you abide with Him. (**John 15:1**)
He loves you so much,
He knows where you will be most effective.

Commit everything you do to the LORD, (**Psalm 37:5**)
Trust in Him,
He will help you with everything,
He will tell you where to begin.

256. Hearing Him Whisper

December 30, 2016

At God's feet
On their knees
Hearing Him whisper
Exactly what they need.

257. Vision

December 30, 2016

Is there a vision on your heart?
An impression that says,
"If this goes far,
Someone is going to deal with more than a simple scar."

Amos received a vision from the Lord, (**Amos 7:1-3**)
God showed him a swarm of locusts,
Eating away the crop,
Amos cried out,
"O Lord God, forgive I pray! Please stop!"

So, the Lord relented,
He heard Amos' plea.
Yes, Amos is a prophet,
But God found an intercessor in he.

Has God showed you something,
That could bring ruin?

Has He given you this vision,
To intercede for the men and women?

258. His Blessings

December 30, 2016

Praise God for His blessings,
He gives so many,
Thankful for His grace, undeserving,
Captured by His love,
Basking in His gaze,
Raising my eyes to see,
Him smiling down on me.

259. Cornerstone

December 30, 2016

The word cornerstone,
Reminds me of community and forgiveness.
Why?
Because Jesus Christ is the cornerstone,
And He was tossed aside as if He were meaningless.
When in fact,
They needed Him more,
Yet He forgave them,
He loved them,

And He continues to intercede for all those, (**Hebrews 7:25**)
Who really need to bow and get their face on the floor.

260. *Prayers On My Heart*

January 2, 2017

I love You, Lord!
Hold me close,
Please place prayers on my heart,
So, the arrows that pierce my heart,
Deflect back to the enemy who throws.

This fight is not against flesh or blood, (**Ephesians 6:12**)
Lord would I see You so close.
The arrows keep coming,
Would my prayers cover those?

Thank You, Lord, for defending me,
For coming down,
Showing the men how they should be,
In the lives of those entrusted by Thee.

We see Your footsteps,
The path marked.
Lord Jesus thank You,
For shining the light on what was dark.

Now we see,
That which was hidden is revealed,
For all to see.
This is the example You want us to be.

Praying on bended knee,
Interceding for others,
While surrendering our personal cares,
To Your authority.

There is a time to speak, (**Ecclesiastes 3:7**)
A time to stay silent,
Lord Jesus teach us when to speak,
Sensitive to Your voice on when to remain silent.

Today, would we fight,
To keep Your name set apart?
Lord Jesus we want Your heart,
So, our prayers leave a mark.

I love You Lord!
Hold me close,
Please place prayers on my heart,
So, the arrows that pierce my heart,
Deflect back to the enemy who throws.

261. *Stepping Into A Life For A Moment*

January 4, 2016

Do we have 5 minutes,
For another?
What if what they need is not big but small?
They need a sister or brother.

A moment in life,
To be a sister or brother,

In another's life,
Meeting a need you see with a God-given eye.

Jesus said He would be pleased,
If we gave a cup of cold water,
To the least of these.
Sometimes that's all they need.

Not something big but small,
A sister or brother stepping into a life for a moment,
Saying "Yes" to Jesus' call,
Wanting to be the one sent.

How many times,
Have we walked the other way?
Missing the moment of need,
Because our eyes are focused on our own self-centered day.
Can we turn around,
Go back,
And pray,
For a second chance,
That very day?

Even if it means waiting in traffic,
Knowing that's how we grow,
When we hear God's voice we go,
Stepping into a life for a moment, not saying "No."

That's life's lesson,
Hearing God's voice,
Above the men and women,
Saying "Yes" when God gives you a choice,
To step in.

Some are stuck on legalistic rules,
Missing the point of life.

The law was satisfied,
When Jesus died.

For by that one offering, (**Hebrews 10:10**)
Jesus forever made perfect and complete,
Those who are being made holy,
Freeing us to be,
His hands and feet,
Whenever He needs.

Did it really cost you that much,
In life,
Those 5 minutes,
When you said "Yes" to God and didn't ask why?

Stepping into a life for a moment,
Is a gift from God, (**James 1:17**)
You may or may never know why He asked you,
That's the grace of God.

262. *Longing On My Heart*

January 6, 2017

There is this longing on my heart,
To be close to the one,
God has set apart—
The one who will love me with all of his heart.

For this man I will wait,
Forever. And. A. Day.

I don't know his name,
But I will wait.

His love for Jesus,
Will set him apart.
His heart before the Lord,
Is not just art.

His pure love,
For Jesus and then me,
Will turn heads,
As people see,
How love is supposed to be.

Love is patient, (**1 Corinthians 13:4**)
Love is kind,
Love lays down his life for his wife,
Calling her "Mine."

Love owns it,
Like no other,
Stepping in quicker,
Than any father, mother, sister or brother.

Love is not jealous— (**1 Corinthians 13:4**)
For it recognizes,
The gifts,
In another's life.
Stepping aside,
To let their spouse shine bright.

Love is not boastful, proud, or rude, (**1 Corinthians 13:4-5**)
But humbles themselves,
Apologizing for their mood.
Knowing it affects their spouse, too.

Love does not demand its own way, (**1 Corinthians 13:5**)
But seeks God and His divine way,
Searching the scriptures for the right path,
Recognizing God is always first, we are last.

Love is not irritable, (**1 Corinthians 13:5**)
It apologizes for that too.
Knowing they themselves,
Bug others too.

Love keeps no record of when it was wronged, (**1 Corinthians 13:5**)
Since I'm the historian,
I'll apologize for that one in a love song.

Love is never glad about injustice, (**1 Corinthians 13:6**)
But rejoices whenever the truth wins out.
Praise God for answered prayer,
Truth stands the test of time beyond a shadow of a doubt. (**Proverbs 12:19**)

Love never gives up, (**1 Corinthians 13:7**)
Never loses faith,
Is always hopeful,
And endures through every circumstance in this Christian race.

Love will last forever, (**1 Corinthians 13:8a**)
Because of Jesus Christ.
The Man who paid the ultimate price,
Freeing us to live the grace of life.

There is this longing on my heart,
To be close to the one,
God has set apart—
The one who will love me with all of his heart.

God makes everything beautiful, (**Ecclesiastes 3:11**)
In its time,
I look forward to the time,
I get to call him "Mine."
Thankful for him in advance,
Praying, "God, please shine your face upon this man." (**Psalm 67:1-2**)

263. The Gospel

January 8, 2017

Thank You Lord for today,
Those moments when You whispered,
"You're going to be ok."

You know my heart,
You know exactly what tore it apart.
That broken heart,
Still has a scar,
But so thankful for You Lord,
For who You truly are.

Your very nature,
Holds me steady.
It's Your character Lord,
The power in Your name alone makes one ready,
To reach the world with those gifts You gave,
Drawing the lost hearts to the One who saves.

Would You fill me with Your Holy Spirit?
So that I can reach the world,
I know I'm just a girl,

But Lord, I need to share the gospel with the world.

We have all fallen short of the glory of God,
No one is perfect,
We deserve more than the rod,
But Jesus Christ came and lived a perfect life,
He died a cruel and torturous death,
So, we can stand ready before God as His Bride.

God is perfect in holiness,
He cannot look upon sin.
The sin you hold within,
Will keep you separated from Him.

You cannot have salvation without repentance.
You need to ask Him for forgiveness to be forgiven.
Don't expect grace,
Be thankful it's given.

It's not just religion,
It's a relationship with the Savior who reigns.
He is on the throne waiting,
But there will be a day when the waiting game ends.

Every knee will bow,
And every tongue will confess,
That Jesus Christ is King,
Would you surrender today the stress,
That is holding you down in suffering.

If you don't bow today,
There will be a day,
You won't have a choice then,
Your eternal destination will already be determined.

There is freedom in this decision,
The choice is yours.
But liberty is truly found,
In Jesus Christ who is knocking at your door. (**Revelation 3:20**)

If you want to accept Jesus Christ into your heart today,
All you have to do is pray,
"Jesus, would You forgive me of my sin,
I recognize You as my Lord and Savior whose blood covers my sin.
Thank you for dying on the cross and rising again.
Please help me to follow you every day of my life amongst these men and women.
Thank You for saving me today, in Jesus' precious name, Amen."

264. My Needs You See

January 12, 2017

My needs You see,
So clearly.

You rescue me.
While I'm on my knees

Lord of my heart,
My heart belongs to Thee.

265. Your Word Is Life

January 15, 2017

Longing for Your voice in my ear,
I sit here reading, praying,
"Lord Jesus, please draw near."

Your word is life,
I need it to fill my life.
I need to know what You want me to do,
So, I sit here listening, waiting for Your cue.

I need to be free to roam,
Filled with the Holy Spirit to reach,
Those in need,
With the message of Jesus Christ, our King.

266. A True Friend

January 15, 2017

What is a true friend?
A true friend,
Steps in.

Covers where their friend is weak,
Making their friend look good,
Not weak.

People have different gifts,
Don't tear your friend down because they don't have your gift.

They are probably stronger than you in another area,
So why are you judging them on wrong criteria?

267. He Cares

January 15, 2017

Life.
Is precious to God.
He cares about every life.
It's love.

268. Oh, My Heart

January 15, 2017

Oh, my heart,
Settle down tonight,
Go to sleep,
Sleep tight,
And in the morning wake,
When it's not yet light,
Knowing God wants to speak,
To your heart at His time.

269. My Soul Silently Waits

January 17, 2017

Truly, my soul silently waits for God; **(Psalm 62:1)**
From Him comes my salvation.
He only is my rock and salvation; **(Psalm 62:2)**
He is my defense,
My fortress where I will never be shaken.

I will face this issue with my eyes focused on God,
Confronting my adversaries,
While trusting God's Sovereignty,
Praising Him for His steadfast love and mercy.

How long will you attack a man? **(Psalm 62:3)**
So many enemies,
All of them trying to kill me if they can,
But they are just a broken down wall I see,
A tottering fence that is unsteady.

They plan to topple me from my high position, **(Psalm 62:4)**
They delight in telling lies about me,
They are friendly to my face in disposition,
But they curse me in their hearts constantly.

For God alone, **(Psalm 62:5)**
O my soul, wait in silence,
Don't complain, be patient,
For my hope is in Him,
Not men or women.

He only is my rock and salvation, (**Psalm 62:6**)
My fortress, my defense,
I will not be shaken,
On God rests my salvation, (**Psalm 62:7**)
My glory and honor come from Him alone,
He is my refuge, a rock where no enemy can reach me with a stone.

Trust in Him at all times you people, (**Psalm 62:8**)
Pour out your heart to Him,
For God is our refuge.
Our safe haven is found solely in Him.

From the greatest to the lowliest— (**Psalm 62:9**)
All are nothing in His sight,
If you weigh them on the scales,
They are lighter than a puff of air, a vapor in the night.

Do not trust in oppression, (**Psalm 62:10**)
Nor vainly hope in robbery,
For oppression holds down a woman or man,
Preventing them from using their gifts accordingly,
While robbery steals unceasingly.

If riches increase,
Do not set your heart on them,
But use them for a good cause,
Remembering they all come from Him.

God has spoken once, (**Psalm 62:11**)
Twice I have heard this:
That power belongs to God,
Not to man who covets it.

To You, O Lord, belongs steadfast love, (**Psalm 62:12**)
For You will render to a man,
According to His work.

270. Awake Out of Sleep

January 17, 2017

Abba! Would You reveal what is corrupt?
Rescue the oppressed,
Deal justice to the oppressor.
Open eyes to the greed in the hearts of those who are already blessed,
Forgive me of my anger.

Help me to be slow to speak, (**James 1:19**)
Because this tongue of mine,
Can deal out too quickly if I don't stop and think.

You see what is wrong,
You see what is causing issues in lives unnecessarily,
Abba! Would You reveal the truth,
And be the safe haven to those who need Your love unconditionally.

Abba! You are my defense,
Thank You for Your perfect knowledge in all of this.
You are able to do even more than I can think, ask, or imagine, (**Ephesians 3:20**)
Here I am Lord, ready for Your plan.

You sent Your Son to die on the cross,
To forgive us of our sins,
The gift You gave, Lord,
Is matchless this side of heaven.

Thank You for Your love displayed,
Would our hearts recognize Hope,
And the sacrifice that came,
In the form of a Man redeeming lives from hell's game.

I love You, God!
Please, regardless of the hardness of men,
Would You send Your people to remind the world of Your love,
Their need for a Savior, and their need to be forgiven?

Would You open eyes to see,
Jesus Christ is returning for those He loves,
Now is the time to awake out of sleep, (**Romans 13:11**)
For our salvation is nearer now than when we first believed.

271. He's Given You Gifts

January 17, 2017

Thank You Lord for knowing me,
For giving me these gifts to meet needs.
I am not perfect, nor will I ever be.
But I'm perfect in Your eyes,
Because You see who I will be,
As You continue transforming me.

No one has arrived yet,
There is still work to be done in all of us.
People can't put a date on someone's purified life,
For only You, God, have the touch.

You purify perfectly,
The old and the young,
We are all in the Refiner's fire,
As You mold us to become,
Ready for Your plan, not man's.

For Your eyes see clearer than any man,
And You alone know the direction of Your plan.

You place passion on a heart,
That is where people should start.
Not doing what they can do obligatory,
But racing passionately past those who don't read Your story.

It's all about You, Lord,
I want to be like Christ.
You've burdened my heart,
To reach the world with the gospel of peace—Jesus Christ.

This is my life,
The gift You've given to me,
Because of the Man who hung on the tree,
I will live fearlessly,
Doing what God has called of me.

Be ready to say no to that which is good,
And yes, to the BEST,
Knowing there isn't time to lose,
Why waste time with that mess?

Jesus is returning,
He's given you gifts,
Don't waste your talents,
Sitting in the man-made pit.

But reach the world,
With the door God opens,
For He alone opens doors no man can shut, (**Revelation 3:7-8**)
And closes doors no man can open.

272. God Loves You

January 17, 2017

God loves you.
He sees your sin.
He knows your heart,
And what you cling to deep within.

He knows your guilt that has you shaken,
He knows your past and the sin that hurt the innocent.
He knows what you said that left a mark,
He knows your anger, bitterness, worry, and fear that has left you in the dark.

You cannot control what comes into the path of your life,
But God knows and will be with you shining the light,
If you repent of your sin,
Recognizing you need Him,
To forgive you of your sin,
He will step in,
And as your Savior alleviate every fear and burden.

You cannot live this life in your own strength,
You cannot get into heaven without His name.
You need Jesus Christ,
To live abundantly in this life,
With His name written across your heart,
Showcasing to all Whose you are.

God loves you.
He sees all the good you do,
In His name,
For His glory,
And He is pleased with you.

Only He can fix the scars,
Caused by your sin,
Trust Him,
To meet the needs of those perfectly,
As He perfectly steps in.

273. Early Will I Seek You

January 19, 2017

O God, You are my God; (**Psalm 63:1**)
Early will I seek You;
My soul thirsts for You;
My flesh longs for You
In a dry and thirsty land,
Where there is no water to be found.

I just want Your Presence,
That's all.
You standing with me,
Through it all.

For when You are with me,
No weapon formed against me, (**Isaiah 54:17**)
Will ever take me down,
For Your strength, O God, is unmatched by those around.

They don't see You,
But I do.
I know You walk with me,
Your Presence has been my glue.

I'm alone in this wilderness,
Wandering the land,
It is so dry Lord,
No springs of water to drink from, it's just sand.

Would You fill me with Your Holy Spirit,
Giving me the Word,
As I seek You early in the morning,
I need Your voice so calming, the cure.

To my aching heart that looks around,
And sees only desert to be found,
Praying for enlightened hearts,
To long for You,
Not settling for where they are,
But desiring a deeper relationship with You.

They have to want it,
You can't force a heart.
You can't make it a law,
Because conformity to a law doesn't conform a heart.

But You Lord transform hearts, (**Romans 12:1-2**)
You meet people right where they are.
You fill them with the Holy Spirit,
You burden their hearts.
In this dry and thirsty land,
I feel like I'm fading,
Losing so much ground,
Wasting.
Away.

But then I see You Lord step in,
Moments when I know it's You.
Bringing back to life,
What was fading from view.

274. The Value Of A Life

January 30, 2017

What's the value of a life?
Jesus Christ's life.

He laid down His life,
To save His Bride.

Would you lay down your life,
To save your Bride,
Knowing what they face,
The constant ridicule, the mocking, the hate?

How do you protect,
What is so sacred?
How do you protect this heart you guard,
From all of this hatred?

Everyone faces something in life,
Who truly understands the scars that abide,
A constant reminder of the pain in life,
Something that never leaves but is constantly in sight.

Anyone that does well,
At anything,
Is subject to the cruel sin,
That surfaces within the one who has no self-discipline.

When you watch your Bride leave others in their dust,
Using the gifts God gave them to impact in the name of Jesus,
Be prepared to lay down your life,
As the sin of others will attack your Bride's life.

What's the value of a life?
Jesus Christ's life.
He set the standard,
Showing us how to truly defend one another.

Our sin separated us from God,
So Jesus stepped in,
He laid down His perfect life,
To make sure we were assured eternity in heaven.

How do you lay down your life,
For the heart you love that is directly in your sight?
You step in while others stare,
No matter what it takes you make sure they know you care.

275. Sitting Here Single

February 4, 2017

Sitting here single,
Knowing I should be working on statistics,
Is it crazy that my prayer for my future man,
Is that he would also be Jesus freakish?

One who takes crazy steps of faith,
That others laugh at,
But then are humbled,
When they see how God elevates my man.

How many times have I stepped out in faith,
Only to be mocked and scorned,
But then You Lord deliver,

And show up those until they mourn,
Over their sin,
And their own failure to step into a situation,
And impact with crazy steps of faith taken.

We all get those moments,
To impact in the name of Jesus Christ,
To step into a situation,
Aligning ourselves with the heart of Christ.

I have so much to learn,
I love watching others,
There will be a day when my man comes into the picture,
While I wait, I watch my sisters and brothers.

But I sit and listen to the Word God speaks to me,
Taking those steps of faith, fearlessly.
Praying for my future man to step into my lane,
So, I can follow him whole-heartedly.

If everyone likes you,
You probably are not standing strong enough in your convictions.
God will burden your heart,
Will you be bold, standing strong on that word in the face of men and women?

The Word you stand on,
Needs to be Christ's words.
You can't make up your own standard,
As that will defeat anyone trying to come up under.

For the words Christ gives,
Are not legalistic.
Jesus Christ satisfied the law,
Everyone can easily follow Him.

People handle things differently,
And that is ok.
Wise is the one who sees,
And gives them room to be.

Sitting here single,
With so much work to do.
Thankful that the Lord to this day,
Has kept men away,
As I truly believe my testimony of purity,
Will bless my future man's heart entirely.

Mock me all you want,
Until you hear from my future beau.
And then challenge me again,
On listening to God, whom I know. (**Jeremiah 9:23-24**)

I have never held a man's hand,
I have never kissed a man,
God said, "Wait to kiss your man,"
So, I'm waiting for my man.
The one who will own it and be my husband.

Stand strong on your convictions,
In the face of those who don't have perfect knowledge,
And God will show the world,
How powerful and awesome HE is.

You can't burden other people with what God asked of you,
Some can't handle it,
But God,
He is with you.

I don't expect,
People to do exactly the same.

But what I know God has asked,
Is for people to walk in holiness every day. (**1 Peter 1:16**)

What God has burdened your heart personally,
As you were abiding with Him continually, (**John 15:1-5**)
If you only knew,
That burden wasn't just to save you.

God knew,
What was up ahead for a few,
And so He told you,
To listen to Him above all of the noise in the room.

Unity is not always correct,
You can unite over something incorrect.
So, I'm sitting here single,
Waiting for the man who would understand the struggle.

As I pray to God,
And read His words,
"Who is a chosen man,
That I may appoint over her?" (**Jer. 50:44b**)

Sitting here single,
I pray,
"Lord show me the man that bears Your image,
That is the man I will follow any day."

I haven't seen him yet.
Don't know where he is.
So, I continue sitting here single,
Doing the work God specifically told me to do that requires me to sit.

Knowing it is as I serve God in the capacity,
He has called of me.

Well, He's just going to drop that man from the sky,
In the path, right in front of me.

I don't want to get an office butt though,
That's what happens when you only sit.
And then God reminds me,
"Alysa, there is a time to run, but seriously there is a time to sit."

And right now, I need to sit,
And do statistics.

276. A Heart To God

February 6, 2017

What is a heart to God?
As He looks into our heart in life,
What is the value to Him?
Jesus Christ.

Does it truly matter what others see,
When their eyes are so blind,
Filled with jealousy?

No.
Because God sees,
And a heart to God,
Is worth eternity.

That's why He sent His only Son,
To redeem the world,
From the sin brought on by one.

To step in,
Defeating the grave,
Conquering the cross,
That dark day.

God made a way,
For your heart to be assured,
Because of Jesus Christ,
Eternity is your heart's worth.

Can we value a heart today?
Scanning and searching to see,
If it meets our standard and needs?
Then tossing it aside when we think,
We can find a better heart up the street.

That attitude in regards to a heart,
Is not of God,
We Christians need to check our heart,
Before God deals His rod.

God specifically formed our heart, (**Psalm 139:13**)
To bare Christ's image.
Why?
Because the world needs to see,
The heart attitude of Jesus in you and me.

When we reflect Christ in any situation,
Those around us stop and see,
A heart redeemed by the precious blood of Jesus Christ, (**1 Peter 1:18-19**)
Who continuously perfects a heart for eternity.

God cares how you handle a heart,
Because He paid a high price for that heart.
He owns it like no other,

So, before you think to analyze a heart,
You better ask permission from God the Father.

What is a heart to God?
What is a heart to you?
Are you aligned with God?
Or do you need to surrender to His eternal view?

277. The Battle On My Heart

February 13, 2017

The battle on my heart,
Is to fight,
To keep Jesus' name set apart.

To many idolize those,
Who can't deliver, restore, or redeem,
Those facing life's woes.

Men and women may be gifted,
Anointed and called,
But they are not God,
They are simply tools chosen to chisel the wall.

They are not perfect,
Some known for their mistakes.
God still loves them,
And uses them for His glory to this day.

Why does God allow us to see,
Those imperfections clearly,

In the men and women,
We once admired and wanted to be?

Those glimpses open our eyes,
To the truth written across the sky.
Who created the heavens and the earth?
God on High.

We worship God alone.
Our praise and petition come,
As we kneel at His throne.

He alone is worthy.
Jesus Christ is God entirely. (**John 10:30**)
When we truly see the Ultimate Man,
Our eyes lose focus as we only see Him.

No one comes close,
Who again gave up their life,
So that we could remain close?
Jesus Christ.

The people God chooses,
Are simply tools in His hand,
To chisel a wall,
Remove the sand.

Desiring to reach the world,
With the message of Good News,
But remember they are imperfect vessels,
Cracked and scarred, yet with the light of Jesus shining through.

God is holy,
Pure and Just,
We worship Him alone,
Knowing we are all but dust.

No one is perfect,
Neither you or I.
Sometimes those scars you wear are reminders that,
There is only One God on High.

Is the battle on your heart,
To fight,
To keep Jesus' name set apart?

278. Worship the LORD in the Beauty of Holiness

February 19, 2017

Elohim,
Please forgive Your church,
For idolizing men and women,
When You alone should be the One heard.

For You are great, (**Psalm 96:4**)
And greatly to be praised,
You are to be feared above all gods,
For You are the sole Deliverer on any given day.

O sheep of His pasture, (**Psalm 95:7**)
Worship the LORD in the beauty of holiness! (**Psalm 96:9**)
Tremble before Him, all the earth,
Honor the LORD's holiness,
Recognizing because of Christ you can enter the throne room, heard.
(**Ephesians 3:12**)

Adonai,
Let Your kingdom praise You,

All the nations of the world,
Uniting together with one voice,
Declaring Your power over the earth!

King,
Let them praise Your great and awesome name— **(Psalm 99:3)**
He is holy.
And forever to be praised.

El Elyon,
You're the Most High God,
You answer our prayers,
Thank you for being the God-Who-Forgives, **(Psalm 99:8)**
Sending Your Son, Christ, to redeem all Your heirs.

O sheep of His pasture **(Psalm 95:7)**
Come and let us worship and bow down **(Psalm 95:6)**
Let us exalt the LORD our God, **(Psalm 99:9)**
And worship at His holy hill where His presence is found; **(Psalm 99:9, Psalm 100:2b)**

Worshiping the LORD in the beauty of holiness, **(Psalm 96:9)**
For the LORD our God is holy. **(Psalm 99:9, Psalm 100:2b)**
O earth! Serve the LORD with gladness, **(Psalm 100:2)**
And sing of His mercy. **(Psalm 101:1)**

279. Jesus Is Returning

February 19, 2017

Jesus is returning,
Are you passionately proclaiming His name?

Wherever you go,
Do people know He came?

Born in a stable,
At the perfect time,
Walking through life flawless,
Ready to redeem mankind.

He's coming again,
To bring us home,
Jesus is returning, friend,
Are you ready? Are your daughters and sons?

Though living life imperfectly,
We should seek to reach and ready,
All those people in our life,
Making sure they are prepared for eternity.

Jesus is returning.

280. Choose To Balance

February 19, 2017

One foot on earth,
One foot in heaven.
How do you balance this thing called life?
When life feels constantly uneven.

I tend to be,
All or nothing in everything.

That doesn't work very well,
When you need to balance life evenly.

Balancing in exercise is easy,
Piece of cake.
You stand on one foot,
While your core strength saves the day.

Balancing life is hard,
When everything in life wants to be first place.
How do you prioritize,
When deadlines loom and stare at you in the face.

As I poured out my complaint to God in prayer,
This is what He whispered in my ear,
"You have to choose to balance,"
Apparently my all or nothing won't work well here.

It is difficult,
That is for sure.
Everyone struggles with balance,
It doesn't matter their position or life adventure.

You cannot compare a life to a life,
Though many like to because it makes them feel better about their life.
What should we do instead but simply recognize,
God has called us to come alongside,
And pray for one another to balance this thing called life.

Choose to balance,
But recognize the gift God gives in rest.
How many times does He allow us to choose?
But remember when He said, "Mary chose the best,"
You should too.

She sat at the Lord's feet,
Over striving and stressing,
You will never regret those sweet moments in His presence,
For everything else has an ending.

But as you sit enjoying Him,
That relationship so dear,
Helps you overcome everything,
It becomes your core strength helping you to endure.

Why do so many fade away,
Because they didn't choose Jesus Christ that day,
They chose instead to work and work,
Putting Jesus off making work their first.

When it is the Lord who blesses anyone's work,
Why do some continue to succeed?
It is the Lord put first.

Prayer and surrender to the Lord each day,
Strengthens one's endurance,
So they are ready to face,
The many challenges that will come in this life of faith.

It's not of this world,
But so needed today.
Yes, we need to choose to balance,
But first we need to place Jesus Christ right in front of our face.

281. A Letter To You

February 22, 2017

If Jesus wrote a letter to you today,
What would it say?

Jesus in the sky,
Writing a letter to His Bride,
"Hear My heart tonight,"

As you sit intently,
Waiting for His words,
Wondering what Jesus is going to speak,
Thinking about your recent actions and your words,
You sit praying, wondering what He thinks.

Everyone's letter might be slightly different,
They alone know where their heart is at,
Yet they may be surprised by what He says,
For He alone knows the true inner heart of every woman and man.

Is He whispering this to you:
"If your heart condemns you,
I am greater than your heart.
I know all things, (**1 John 3:20**)
Believe Me, I know right where you are."

Or,
"You are My masterpiece,
Created anew in Me,
So that you can do,
All of the good things I have planned for you." (**Ephesians 2:10**)

Some promises He whispers,
As His letter is heaven sent.
But then again there are also those words,
That need to be listened to closely with intent.

"You have left your first love, (**Revelation 2:4**)
Return to Me.
Why has your heart wandered so far,
Do you still love Me?"

"Your recent actions show,
You've been putting on a show,
Placing others first before Me,
When I am the One who set you free."

"I know all the things you do, (**Revelation 2:2**)
I have seen your hard work and patient endurance.
I know you don't tolerate evil,
You examine all to reveal it."

"But I desire your love,
Not your works.
Your cold mechanical heart,
Needs a rebirth."

To some He may address,
Their lack of love,
But to the persecuted,
He pours out His love.

"I know your works, (**Revelation 2:9**)
I know your suffering,
I know your poverty,
But you are rich in the fellowship of suffering. (**Revelation 2:9, Ephesians 3:8-10**)

"For I endured,
More than you ever will, (**Hebrews 2:18**)
This is just a taste,
As you experience what I suffered in your place."

"I know the slander of those opposing you, (**Revelation 2:9-10**)
But don't be afraid of what you are about to suffer.
The Devil will throw some of you in prison to put you to the test,
You will be persecuted for 10 days, no less.
Remain faithful to Me above the rest when facing death,
And I will give you the crown of life, the BEST."

"Don't worry,
I will also punish those who persecuted you,
In proportion to the suffering they caused you. (**Jeremiah 25:14**)
Keep going, I love you."

Jesus' words cut into our inner most thoughts and desires,
Showing us who we are. (**Hebrews 4:12**)
His whispered words penetrate our hearts,
As He alone sets the bar.
Then reveals how far,
He went to redeem us from hell's death star. (**Isaiah 14:12-15, Revelation 20:10**)

To others the Lord may write,
"I know your loyalty and faithfulness,
Even while living in that place,
Where Satan's throne is. (**Revelation 2:13**)
But you compromise by not correcting,
The sin in your midst. (**Revelation 2:14-15**)
Repent or else they will now,
Fight against the sword in My mouth." (**Revelation 2:16**)

"Don't try to fit in with the world,
That wants you to be ok with their view of the world.
They will only bring you down,
What they need from you is to stand firm on the only solid ground."
(**Matthew 7:24-26**)

"Those victorious,
Will get a new name for this,
Written on a white stone,
No one will know the name,
Except the one who receives it for their own." (**Revelation 2:17**)

To others Jesus may write,
"Remember when I shared with you all,
That I am One with My Father, (**John 10:30**)
I am God and I laid down My life for all." (**John 3:16**)

Jesus then with eyes as bright as flames of fire, (**Revelation 2:18**)
Purifying those in His church,
For is not God's glory only witnessed,
In a pure church?

Purity is a light to the world, (**Matthew 5:16**)
For it is unlike the world.
But God's glory will be removed suddenly, (**Ezekiel 10:18**)
From a church filled with idolatry and immorality.

"I know all the things you do, (**Revelation 2:19**)
Your love, your faith, and your patient endurance.
And I see your constant improvement,
In all of this.
But this I have against you,
You and your church are not walking in holiness, (**Revelation 2:20**)
And you are allowing it.
I don't want this in My midst.
Correct this."

"Unrepentant sin will be judged, (**Revelation 2:22, Romans 6:23**)
I don't play with this.
Repent and turn from your sin today, (**Matthew 3:8, Ezekiel 18:32**)
And live."

"Now there are a few who set themselves apart, (**Revelation 2:24-28**)
Purposing in their heart,
To these I will allow to rule and reign with Me,
In the here and now."

As Jesus whispers His letter,
There are so many words to consider,
Some are encouraging while others correct,
But there is a direct word for whom the letter is sent.

"I know all the things you do, (**Revelation 3:1**)
And that you have a reputation for being alive,
But you are spiritually dead,
My glory has left."

"Wake up and strengthen what little remains, (**Revelation 3:2**)
For even that is at the point of being spiritually dead.
Your deeds are far from being right in my sight.
Repent."

"Go back to what you heard and believed at first, (**Revelation 3:3**)
Cling to it firmly,
Turn to Me again,
Or else I will come upon you suddenly."

"There are some who have not soiled their garments, (**Revelation 3:4**)
With evil deeds.
They will walk with me in white,
For they are worthy.
All who are victorious will be clothed in white, (**Revelation 3:5**)
I will never erase their names from the Book of Life,
I will announce before My Father and the angels that they are Mine."

Another whispered word,
From the One who is holy and true, (**John 14:6, Revelation 3:7**)
The One who holds the key,
Who shuts doors no man can shut, for you,
And opens doors no man can open, He does it so easily.

"I know all the things you do, (**Revelation 3:8**)
And I have opened a door just for you,
That no one can shut.
For I know all that you have gone through."

"You had little strength, (**Revelation 3:8**)
Yet you obeyed My word,
You didn't deny Me,
But clung to My word."

"Those liars, (**Revelation 3:9**)
I will take care of,
They will come to you,
They will acknowledge that it is you whom I love."

"Because you have obeyed, (**Revelation 3:10**)
My command to persevere,
I will protect you from the great time of testing,
Do not fear."

"Look! I am coming quickly, (**Revelation 3:11**)
Hold onto what you have tightly,
Let no one can take away your crown,
Walk victoriously!" (**Revelation 3:12**)

So many words to love and hold dear,
Even those words of correction,
At least correct so clear,
Drawing one near.

"I know all the things you do, (**Revelation 3:15**)
That you are neither hot nor cold.
You are like lukewarm water,
That I want to spit out of my mouth because its old."

"You say so many things, (**Revelation 3:17-18**)
But you are wrong.
I advise you to read My word,
So, you will know where true worth comes from."

"I am the One who corrects and disciplines, (**Revelation 3:19, Hebrews 12:5**)
Everyone I love.
Be diligent and turn from your indifference.
For it is you that I love."

"Look! Here I stand at the door and knock, (**Revelation 3:20**)
If you hear Me calling and open the door,
I will come in so that we can talk,
And we can share a meal as friends, strengthening your core." (**Revelation 3:20, Psalm 119**)

Tonight,
What did Jesus whisper to your heart,
As He called you to abide?

282. My Heart So Heavy

February 23, 2017

With my heart so heavy,
Weighed down,

I don't know what to do,
But pray, "Lord, please take this now."

I can't work on the projects I'm supposed to,
The homework is set aside,
As my heart remains stuck in a moment,
Needing a heart transformation tonight. (**Ezekiel 36:26**)

Even if I got a new heart,
The memories remain,
Why do I have to be a historian?
Loving every detail of every day.

And as I sit whispering my prayers,
I hear the Lord whisper back,
"Do not fear, (**Luke 12:32**)
I will make up for what you lack."

283. Words of Life Are Redeeming

February 24, 2017

As I sit here early in the morning,
Reading God's Word,
His Words of life are redeeming,
And I'm drawn to Him with even more fervor.

Obedience to God over man,
Is so important in this land.
It's time to take a stand,
And stand strong on those God given convictions,
That impact our land.

I have to obey God.
Plain and simple.
As I sit here reading **Jeremiah 35,**
God asks, "Why did you obey man over My principle?"

Can you imagine God asking that question to you?
Is there something He's been asking you to do?
Yet you have held back,
Because a man said not to?

God's Word is Sovereign,
He remains in control.
He is all knowing,
So when He says, "Go," you go.

284. *Life.*

February 24, 2017

My book of poems— Life,
All describe aspects of heroic endurance,
What to do in life,
When we are constantly tested under trial and strife.

God blesses the people, (**James 1:12**)
Who patiently endure testing,
Who endure temptation,
Who remain steadfast under trial,
Holding fast to Christ;
Those will be the ones who receive the crown of life.

The reward for enduring,
Clinging to Christ,
Is Life.

Many succumb and cave amidst the battle,
The temptations are strong,
The testing making one feel unstable,
Moving them to bail,
When God wants them to remain able.

But those who patiently endure,
Persevering in prayer,
The reward is Life,
Eternal Life is theirs.
That's the gift,
Given by Christ,
Every crown describes,
A characteristic of the afterlife,
And this crown for enduring trial,
Is the Crown of life.
Eternal life.

There will be a day,
When you cast that crown Christ's way.
Recognizing it was solely Jesus,
Who gave you the strength to endure the day.

Jesus Christ reigns,
He gives strength to all,
Who seek Him above all,
He hears and answers every call.

So, I encourage you today,
When times of trial come your way,
Cling to Christ and His Word,
As Jesus' precious name and presence answers,

Every overwhelming trial,
Becoming your greatest treasure.

285. *That One*

March 1, 2017

As I sit here,
Overwhelmed with life,
I'm reminded of that one God called me to pray for,
He walked right by me without even saying "hi" or "bye."
Then I never saw him again.
I didn't know why,
God called me to pray for him,
So I asked God why,
And well those details are between me and Him.
Some prayers are best left unspoken.
Because there are too many nosey men and women.

286. *Share Jesus Christ*

March 5, 2017

When you share Jesus Christ,
In the secular workplace,
Know this,
God is with you in that place.

The key is to have no regrets,
Share with everyone and anyone,
Pray for the unsaid.
Speak into their life,
Share the gospel with those who are going the wrong way,
Pray for their salvation every time they step into the place.

You never know when your day there will end,
So, have no regrets friend.
God placed you there for a reason,
It could just be for a season,
There are many He wants you to speak to,
He has given you words of life, the Good News.

So many need Jesus,
They won't enter a church,
You might be the only one,
To give them the truth of God's Word.

There is a time for everything,
A season for everything under the sun.
God is the holder of time,
You just run when He says run.

You share what Jesus Christ spoke to you,
His every whisper to your heart,
Is also a whisper for their heart.
They may only get it from you,
So, step into the place God prepared for you.

You may never know,
The impact of your faithfulness,
To reach those,
Others left alone in their mess.

Have no regrets,
In life.
Don't worry,
As you share Jesus Christ,
Many will then experience the true meaning of life.

God will place you where you will be,
Most effective for Him.
There is a time for everything,
Every season belongs to Him.

Redeem the time,
For the days are evil,
People need to hear about Jesus Christ,
So, share words of life.

God may move some,
So others can step into place,
It's a passing of the baton,
It's a call to step into the shoes and run the race.

Jesus Christ saves,
There are many in need.
Will you be the work missionary,
Ready with eyes to see,
And a heart to reach,
Those in need?

287. A New Beginning

March 7, 2017

A new beginning,
A fresh slate,
Starting life anew,
Prepared for whatever God brings this day.

I love the Lord, (**Psalm 116:1-2**)
Because He hears and answers my prayers,
He bends down to listen to me,
So, I will pray all day every day for the rest of my years.

There are times,
When the Lord moves you on,
Recognize those moments,
And thank Him for His perfect knowledge over all.

A new beginning,
Is good,
Sometimes the Lord takes something away,
So, you can stop focusing on what is good,
To focus on the best all day every day.

For myself right now,
I don't know what that best is yet,
So, I sit and bow,
Utterly dependent upon God,
For the here and now.

There will be a day,
When I see,
The reasons why God changed my scenery,
But until that day,

I will simply obey,
Simply loving the fact,
God bends down to listen to me. (**Psalm 116:2**)

288. *What Do You Want Me To Pray For?*

March 7, 2017

Abba!
What do you want me to pray for today?
As I sit here waiting for Your ok.
You have me here for a reason,
I don't want to waste this season.
As I look all around me,
I see mothers with children sometimes screaming.
I love it.
And I want it.
But I don't have it.
Yet.
So there is a reason,
For this season,
Of isolation,
I've already prayed for the nation,
What else is important to You today?

I think I need to make a list,
Of those needs that truly exist.
So, thankful for Your touch on my life,
As that is the only reason why,
I am able to do,
What You are calling me to do.

Praying for my future family,
And those children that will drive me crazy.
I can't wait,
I'm probably going to be as big as a house during those pregnant days.
But seriously,
I've been waiting forever for that day.
Literally.

I absolutely want many,
Playing with my children,
Will be the best gift given,
Third of course to Jesus, and then my husband.

So, I watch families now;
Wondering what it will be like then.
FYI to my future husband,
Daddy-daughter day at work is going to happen;
And Father-son day is a must and a given.

One of the best gifts to children,
Is watching Dad and Mom in action,
Living life,
Fearlessly for Christ.

What do I desire in my future marriage and family?
For my family to serve Jesus entirely,
Using their gifts to reach many,
It doesn't matter a person's age or responsibility,
For every person is called to live life honoring the King.

The joy a child brings to a life,
Seeing their eyes sparkle as they want to hide,
And have you find them,
Their giggles are awesome.

So, Abba, I sit here praying,
For that day,
I meet that man You have set apart for me,
Wondering what life will be like,
When we serve You King, as a family.

289. Praying through Psalm 116:

For That Man I've Yet To Meet
March 7, 2017

Abba!
Right now my heart is overly burdened to pray,
For that man I have yet to meet,
You forgot to tell me what day.
Or who You want to hold my key.

So I pray,
Though it's hard when I don't know the details.
How am I supposed to pray specifically,
When I have no idea his needs.

I try to be sensitive to Your voice,
But I am not perfect.
So, I sit here reading through Your Word,
Trusting right where I am at is what is perfect.

I pray he loves You, (**Psalm 116:1**)
Knowing You hear his voice,
You bend down to hear his prayers, (**Psalm 116:2**)
Oh, would he please keep praying seeking You above all the noise.

If he is experiencing sorrow, (**Psalm 116:3**)
Would he call upon Your name, (**Psalm 116:4**)
"Please Lord save me!"
Knowing with full assurance You will enter the game.

Abba, would he recognize,
How kind You are, (**Psalm 116:5**)
How good You are,
So, merciful this God of ours!
The LORD protects with His power, (**Psalm 116:6a**)
Those of childlike faith, every hour.

Was he facing death? (**Psalm 116:6b**)
Abba, that scares me,
But I will pray for the unsaid.
There are different types of deaths,
Could it be a friendship or something else instead?

But You bring dead things back to life, (**John 11:43-44**)
It's in Your Word,
So, Abba, would You raise the dead,
And bring back to life its worth.

You meet a need,
For You truly see,
So, I will thank You in advance,
For the protection You have given to this man.

Would he see how You have saved him,
Would he rest again, (**Psalm 116:7**)
You LORD have been good to him.

Thank You for saving him from death, (**Psalm 116:8**)
His eyes from tears,
His feet from stumbling,
You rescued him from all his fears.

Would he walk in Your presence, (**Psalm 116:9**)
Every day of his life,
Knowing You will deliver,
At the perfect time.

You heard his voice, (**Psalm 116:10**)
His cry in the dark,
He believed and therefore he spoke,
His prayers were heard in the car.

Have men lied to him? (**Psalm 116:11**)
Did they say they would be there for him?
Yet failing to reach him?
I will pray for them.

But thank You LORD,
For You were there.
You delivered him,
From every fear.

Abba, would You speak to his heart today,
As he asks You what he can offer You, (**Psalm 116:12**)
For You have done so much for him,
Would he wait patiently for Your cue.

Would he lift up a cup symbolizing his salvation; (**Psalm 116:13**)
Would he praise the LORD's name for saving him?
I know he will keep his promises to You, LORD, (**Psalm 116:14**)
In the presence of all Your people all over the world.
Thank You LORD for delivering him,
Thank You for moving on behalf of him,
Going before him,
Parting the red sea just for him.

You love him LORD,
I know You do.
He loves You too.

Your loved ones are precious to You, (**Psalm 116:15**)
It grieves You when they die.
Would he ask You, LORD, what he can do for You,
To help those suffering even when he cannot explain to them why.

O LORD, he is Your servant. (**Psalm 116:16**)
This humble man,
The son of Your handmaid,
Thank You for freeing him.

I know he is thankful, (**Psalm 116:17**)
Endless thanks to You, LORD,
He will keep his promises, (**Psalm 116:18**)
Even when those promises hurt.
In the presence of Your people,
In the house of the LORD, (**Psalm 116:19**)
Praise the LORD!

I don't know who this man is,
I'm not sure if this prayer,
Would have made his prayer list,
But I'm thankful for him while wondering where,
In the world he is.

I would hug him if I could,
So, a bear hug from afar.
I have no idea who he is,
Oh Abba, please guard my heart.

290. *That Whisper*

March 12, 2017

That whisper to my heart,
"I want you seeking Me now, (**Jeremiah 29:13**)
With all of your heart."
Draws my heart,
To the One who truly knows,
My heart,
Transforming my stone-cold heart, (**Ezekiel 36:26**)
Into that soft moldable heart,
That one can talk to,
Any day.

291. *Jesus—The Cornerstone*

March 13, 2017

Jesus,
You are the Cornerstone,
You set the foundation for many,
Yet You were rejected by most,
When You wanted them standing strong, ready.

Some tossed You aside,
When You wanted to be walking by their side.
Some looked the other way,
When You wanted them looking to You, that day.

Some opened another book,
When You wanted them opening Your book.

They sought wisdom from man,
When You wanted them seeking You above any man.

Why are some washed to and fro?
When the winds and rain come,
They leave and go,
Unable to withstand, wanting only the shining sun.

They cannot endure,
The trial or storm,
That comes into every life,
They resist, looking for the door.

And yet, had they been abiding with You,
Built on the rock,
They would have clearly witnessed You,
Moving into situations, rescuing them with the words, "Let's talk."

There is a difference,
Between running away from the storm,
And being rescued in the midst,
Delivered by God's strong arm.

Lord, had they only sought You first,
Your heart,
Your words,
They would have remained firm in this spiritual war.

You are the only One,
That knows,
What will come into every life,
Seriously, no one else knows.

So, it's the call to abide,
To put You first,

Recognizing You deliver,
You do not want people unnecessarily hurt.

You are the Cornerstone,
No one will ever have a strong structure of people,
Walking in unity,
Unless You are the foundation holding the people,
Steady.

Jesus, my prayer today,
Is that people would turn to You first,
Recognizing they need a Savior,
They need a Deliverer,
A Rock of Refuge,
A Conqueror,
They need the Cornerstone—You.

292. My Comfort

March 15, 2017

This is my comfort, (**Psalm 119:50a NKJV**)
In my affliction,
Your word, Lord,
Heals every situation.

For Your word, (**Psalm 119:50b NKJV**)
Has given me life.
It touches my heart,
Every time I abide.

I can't explain it,
But it's true,
How is it that when I sit before You,
The enemy is subdued?

The issues so pressing,
Don't necessarily stop,
But Your presence assures me,
You are on the throne and the enemy is not.

You give me new insight,
Into every situation,
You comfort my heart,
With Your words so clearly spoken.

"Go into all the world, (**Matthew 28:19**)
And make disciples of men,
Preach the gospel, (**Mark 16:15**)
Encouraging people to pray, enduring to the end."

293. *Praying Relentlessly*

March 15, 2017

Jesus, You know what I need,
To bring me peace,
In this situation,
That has brought me to my knees.

I will keep praying,
Relentlessly,

Knowing You are Sovereign,
Over everything.

Thank You Lord,
For meeting with me,
In this very moment,
Of my need.

For You showed up,
And comforted me,
When I was weak,
Needing to see.

294. The LORD Builds

March 20, 2017

Unless the LORD builds the house, (**Psalm 127:1a**)
They labor in vain who build it.
Unless the LORD builds the community,
The work of the builders is useless.

Unless the LORD guards the city, (**Psalm 127:1b**)
The watchman stay awake in vain.
Best to pray and ask God to lead,
The safety and security showing exactly the need.

It is useless for you to work so hard, (**Psalm 127:2**)
From early morning until late at night,
Anxiously working for food to eat;
For God gives rest to his loved ones every night.

Behold, children are a heritage from the LORD, **(Psalm 127:3)**
The fruit of the womb is a reward.
Like arrows in the warrior's hand, **(Psalm 127:4)**
So are the children born to a man.

How happy is the man, **(Psalm 127:5)**
Whose quiver is full of them!
He will not be put to shame,
When he confronts his accusers at the city gates.

295. *Tunnel of Life*

March 21, 2017

Kids hold their breath,
As the car goes through the tunnel.
Making faces, trying not to laugh,
Believing they are able.

The tunnels in life,
However, hit us by surprise.
The moment makes our breath catch,
And we fail to breathe hoping it won't last.

It's dark,
Can't always see the light at the end.
Every tunnel in life,
Has its own length, God determined.

Moments when we fail to breathe,
And we recognize God entering the scene.

So quickly He takes us in His arms,
Breathing life into our body, turning wounds into scars.

Reminders of when,
He entered in.
Never leaving us to face,
That dark tunnel we hate.

As kids we play games,
But when we grow up we see,
Life is more than a game,
And every scar tells a story.

A story of when,
God entered in.
Changing the dark tunnel of life,
Into a story showcasing the miracle of Jesus' resurrection.

Life beyond the grave,
Life for eternity, He saves.
Jesus is the only way,
Into the Father's arms today.

296. Life Is A Journey

March 21, 2017

Your life is a journey free from the law,
As you travel with a deep consciousness of God, (**1 Peter 1:18 MSG**)
Recognizing He paid a ransom for your life, (**1 Peter 1:18 NLT**)
With the precious lifeblood of Jesus Christ. (**1 Peter 1:19 NLT**)

The sinless, spotless, Lamb of God, (**1 Peter 1:19 NLT**)
Destroyed the law,
That kept you far from God.

God chose Him for this purpose, (**1 Peter 1:20 NLT**)
Long before the world began.
God did this for you, (**1 Peter 1:20b NLT**)
So that you could be born again. (**1 Peter 1:23a NLT**)

This new life will last forever,
Because it comes from the eternal, living Word of God. (**1 Peter 1:23b NLT**)
The future starts now,
As we recognize Jesus Christ on the cross.

"Be holy for I am."
God declares.
Eight times in scripture,
Do we hear?

Our journey in life,
Must be shaped by God's life, (**1 Peter 1:15 MSG**)
A life blazing with holiness,
Set apart for Jesus Christ.

297. Praise Him!

March 24, 2017

Praise the name of the LORD, (**Psalm 135:1**)
Praise Him!
All you who serve in the house of the LORD,

In the courts of the house of our God. (**Psalm 135:2 NLT**)
Praise the LORD! (**Psalm 135:3 NLT**)

For the LORD is good,
Celebrate His wonderful name with music, (**Psalm 135:3 NLT**)
For the LORD is good.

Oh, bless the LORD,
All you servants of the LORD, (**Psalm 134:1 NLT**)
Who by night stand in the house of the LORD! (**Psalm 134:1b NKJV**)
Lift up your hands in holiness, (**Psalm 134:2a NLT**)
And bless the LORD. (**Psalm 134:2b NKJV**)

May the LORD,
Who made heaven and earth,
Bless you from Jerusalem, (**Psalm 134:3 NLT**)
For you have been heard.

Your name, O LORD, endures forever,
Your fame, O LORD, throughout all generations. (**Psalm 135:13 NKJV**)
You who fear the LORD, bless the LORD, (**Psalm 135:20b NKJV**)
For the LORD's name is magnified in all the nations.

298. Don't Stop Praying

March 25, 2017

Don't stop praying,
Your prayers are heard,
Keep persevering in prayer,
And God will strengthen your world.

As you wait,
Patiently persevering in prayer,
Longing for the answer,
God will meet you right there.

For those who wait upon the Lord, (**Isaiah 40:31**)
He renews their strength,
He takes care of it Himself,
Making sure those go the length.

They shall mount up with wings like eagles,
Soaring through the crowd,
They shall run and not be weary,
Solely because they bow down.

They shall walk and not faint,
Recognizing when to slow down,
Seeing God's hand guide every step,
Knowing what to pick up and what to put down.

299. Would You?

April 2, 2017

Holy Spirit, would You come rest upon me,
And fill me?
So I can share Jesus' name,
Relentlessly.

For I am not ashamed of the gospel, (**Romans 1:16**)
It is the power of God,

So many need Jesus Christ,
Right now in this world.

Father, would You smile upon me,
And say "Yes" to my plea?
I need to share Jesus' name,
I need to decrease.

Jesus, would You meet with me.
I need Your presence so much,
I feel alone,
I need Your touch.

300. *God Is Faithful*

April 2, 2017

When we say,
"God is faithful,"
What do we mean?
Is it a characteristic that is loyal?
Or is it more than that as it magnifies the unseen?

He never leaves us,
Nor forsakes us, (**Hebrews 13:5**)
For He is the Good Shepherd, opening the door, (**John 10:11,
Revelation 3:8**)
Guiding us through life to eternity's shore. (**Revelation**)

When we are faithless,
He remains faithful still. (**2 Timothy 2:13**)

When we are struggling to believe issues will change,
He calls us "little faith," as we question His will (**Matthew 8:26**)

Jesus cannot deny Himself,
He will never change (**Malachi 3:6, Hebrews 13:8**)
All of His promises,
Are backed by the power of His name.

So when we say,
"God is faithful,"
Those three little words carry so much weight,
As we share with the world the meaning of Jesus' name.

He will never change. (**Malachi 3:6, Hebrews 13:8**)
He is the One constant in your life.
His death on the cross took your place,
Showing He will always love you for faithfulness is His very name.

301. *You Know My Heart*

April 19, 2017

Oh Lord,
You know my heart,
The reminders that hold me down,
When I want to go far.

Forgive me Lord,
For letting it affect me.
I know I get to choose,
I'm thankful You are the one Who gets me.

You are the Savior of my soul,
I love You so much,
Lord, You redeem it all,
I'm just waiting for Your touch.

These current issues in life,
Won't last long.
However, there will be a new issue tonight.

For isn't that life?
There is always something.
It's how we handle the issue,
When it is so pressing.

Do we take it to You,
Revealing every ounce of our heart?
Letting You deal with it all,
As You then speak to our heart.

For seriously,
You are the only One,
Who deals with things perfectly.

You know us.
You love us.
Then You correct us.
Then You love us.

Then we learn
How to handle the next issue that comes.
Better with each turn.

302. Sweetspot

April 21, 2017

I miss my sweetspot.
But as I think looking back,
It was just a dot,
Among many that will come and go pretty fast.

For isn't that life?

Once you get settled in,
Or you could have been there awhile,
The fruit is flowin',
And then the shears come cutting.

Pruning for more growth,
Is what God does best,
In the life He gives,
To all of us.

Do you think God wants you,
To have more crowns than even you desire?
You could be content with what you have,
But He wants you to go farther.

So often we don't understand,
When our life gets pruned.
Something gets cut away,
And we wonder why we were moved.
Or why that was taken away,
When wasn't it a good thing that day?

The vine holds the nourishment that feeds the fruit,
The vinedresser prunes in the perfect season,

Cutting back the vine at the moment it needs it to.
For if the vine were never cut,
The branches wouldn't grow but would remain stuck.
This isn't seen with the visible eye,
For only the One who knows the vine can share the reason as to why.

For every plant has its own season,
Every fruit feeds specific people.
The plants are different,
Can't be treated the same,
The vinedresser knows His plants,
And prunes them the right way.

If a branch does not bear fruit,
The Lord cuts it off.
The nourishment in the branch,
Is getting wasted on what?

But so too,
If the branch bears much fruit,
The branch is pruned in view,
To bare even more fruit to feed more than a few.

To bear fruit,
You need to abide.
Abide with Jesus,
Every morning, noon, and night.

Sit and talk with Him,
Listen too.
He has so much,
That He wants to tell you.

He wants to share His heart,
Regarding you.

He loves you so much,
Will you love Him too?

How can you best love Jesus?
Well now that's up to you,
He will whisper words to your heart,
On how He wants to receive love from you.

Abide.
When you abide,
It truly is a sweet ride.
A journey in time,
Adventures all of the time.

Even when the shears come,
And the cutting trims away more than some,
And you feel like you lost your sweetspot,
Just wait,
It will come.

Keep abiding,
Recognizing,
The fruit that comes,
Is feeding more than one.

This life is not about you,
It's about Jesus,
His story told through you.

How does your life
Best describe,
Jesus Christ,
The man who suffered and died,
Providing eternal life?

Jesus declares, "I am the true vine,
And My Father is the vinedresser."
Jesus is your nourishment all of the time,
The fruit you bear,
Reflects His name, not yours, not mine.

303. *That Burden*

April 26, 2017

That burden that won't leave,
Is an invitation from the King,
Calling you in,
To His presence.

Will you kneel at His feet,
Surrendering everything?
The burden, the care.
He wants you to leave it there.

Not to a man,
But to Him alone.
For He carries the burdens,
While He sits on His throne.

He cares for you personally, (**1 Peter 5:7**)
Your needs He sees so clearly.
Jesus, Your King,
Is smiling.

His face shines when you enter in,
Loving your presence.

As you kneel pouring out your heart and soul,
He knows love purifies gold.
So, He loves on you,
As He hears you whisper your heart,
"I want to decrease Lord,
So, people can see who You truly are."

"This life is not about me,
It's about You,
This journey,
I pray reflects You in truth."

His face illuminates,
As He looks upon you,
Adoration and grace,
Lingers in His voice as He tells you,
"Go reach more than a few.
I'll take these burdens freeing you,
From those chains not designed for you."

The immediate relief will flood your soul,
As you step into the world, oh so bold,
Not ashamed of the gospel of Christ,
For Jesus is the answer to every issue in this life.

That burden that won't leave,
Is an invitation from the King,
Calling you in,
To His presence.

He wants to talk to you,
To hear your voice,
He loves you more than you even know,
Your presence makes His face glow.

304. *Help, Help!*

May 5, 2017

I cry out to You,
Do you see me?
Help, help!
I need Your strength fearlessly.

This is over my head,
I don't know what to do.
My failure is ringing,
It's ringing oh so true.

Everything looks bleak,
Mockers are everywhere,
People tell me what to seek,
They say things but I wonder if they really care.

Situations out of my control,
Have hit my world.
I'm isolated and alone,
Because no one truly understands my world.

And it's that, really.
They don't understand,
What I care about so dearly.
For they are isolated from that reality.

I'm not backing down,
I still have fight left,
But help, help!
I need to know where to cast my net.

Do I throw it to the other side?
Do I look to the left?
Do I look to the right?
Or take two steps to the side?

I'm weakened,
Exhausted,
But strengthened,
Solely because of the Man who went ahead.

The Man who took it all,
Without waiting for a call.
He died on that tree,
For me.
He took my place,
Experiencing all of the hate,
Oh, the grace,
That washes over me today.

I'm so thankful for Him.
He's given me the strength,
For He endured affliction,
Showing me how to deal with today.

Jesus Christ is His name,
The Savior of all,
He loves you too,
He'll rescue you when you're backed against a wall.

305. Purifying

May 5, 2017

There are certain things,
We have to do our self.
But there are other things,
Where we need help.

Purifying,
Is a self-issue.
Purify yourself, (**1 John 3:3**)
And ask God to examine you. (**Psalm 139:23-24**)

Oh, let the evil of the wicked, (**Psalm 7:9**)
Come to an end,
And may You, Lord, establish the righteous,
As You test their hearts and minds in perfection.

For You alone have perfect sight,
Into every situation,
As You examine everyone in the dark night,
Showcasing those with true adoration.

What does that look like,
Oh Lord,
That moment You examine,
And reveal someone's worth?

Can we even explain,
How You move and reveal a name?
You know hearts,
No two hearts are the same.
You Who know hearts, (**Acts 15:8**)
Acknowledge a heart,

By giving the Holy Spirit,
Taking one far.

All for Your glory,
For You alone do the work,
You are the Creator,
You are the One saying, "Go into all the world." (**Matthew 28:19**)

The thing with people,
In their natural human state,
They get stuck on the rules,
Forgetting You died and gave grace.

They give grace,
When they want to give grace,
But go legalistic,
When they want a point made.

And yet, Lord, You test the righteous, (**Psalm 11:5**)
Because You love the righteous. (**Psalm 11:7**)
And You Lord have tested us.
You love us.

Your words alone, are pure words. (**Psalm 12:6**)
Refined in a furnace of earth.
Your perfect voice,
Tests our imperfect world.

306. The Wedding

May 22, 2017

The wedding of the King, **(Psalm 45, Revelation 19, 2 Peter 3:9)**
Is coming,
His anointed words,
Alleviate the suffering.

He stands amidst the crowd,
Drawing people to Himself even now,
Not missing a chance,
To reach the lost in the land.

Humility surrounds You, O King,
Grace is on Your lips, **(Psalm 45:2)**
God has blessed You forever, **(Psalm 45:2)**
For You reflect Him.

Victory is Yours,
As You defend truth, humility and righteousness. **(Psalm 45:4)**
Your arrows hit the heart's target, **(Psalm 45:5)**
Defeating all opposition.

Your throne, O God, is forever and ever, **(Psalm 45:6)**
Your royal power is expressed in justice,
For You love righteousness, **(Psalm 45:7)**
And hate wickedness.

Therefore, God, Your God, **(Psalm 45:7)**
Has anointed You, **(Psalm 45:7)**
With the oil of gladness, **(Psalm 45:7)**
More than Your companions. **(Psalm 45:7)**

Listen to me, O royal daughter, (**Psalm 45:10**)
Take to heart what I say. (**Psalm 45:10**)
Forget your people (**Psalm 45:10**)
And your homeland far away. (**Psalm 45:10**)

For your Royal Husband delights in your beauty, (**Psalm 45:11**)
You've captured Him with your love,
Draw near to Him now,
And experience true love.

Love is found in Him,
So your love will grow more perfect, (**1 John 4:17**)
As you dwell with Him,
Becoming more like Him.

Your sons will become kings, (**Psalm 45:16**)
Like their father, (**Psalm 45:16**)
Ruling the land, (**Psalm 45:16**)
While your daughters,
Reach the lost with words clearly spoken.

This abundant life lived,
In honor of the One,
Who gives,
Knowing home,
Is where life begins.

307. *Will You Smile?*

May 22, 2017

Will You smile, (**Psalm 67:1**)
At me?
Shining Your face,
For all to see?

So that I can go,
Into all the world,
Making Your way known, (**Psalm 67:2**)
Throughout the earth.

308. *In A Blink*

May 26, 2017

Life.
In a blink of an eye,
Passes by.
How many days, months, years,
Go by,
And you failed to remember why,
You're here?

309. *Praying For You*

May 26, 2017

I haven't talked to you,
But I have been thinking about you.
Praying for you,
That the Lord would fill you,
Afresh with His love,
So there would be an outpouring from above,
Spilling onto everyone around,
Touching hearts with the sweet sound,
"Jesus loves you."

310. *His Decision*

May 26, 2017

The Lord has recently,
Blessed me,
With time.

I didn't realize at that time,
How stressed and overburdened I was,
Until the Lord sweetly made a decision,
And I experienced the drastic change of situations.

My eyes are opened to how unhealthy it was,
And so I thank the Lord,
For seeing from above,
What my eyes failed to see,
Oh, to see with eyes of love.

There are times when you don't think,
You just do the next thing.
Failing to see,
How unhealthy,
Life can be.

Time passes by so quickly,
That if you are constantly just doing the next thing,
You may fail to see,
Your true need,
Until the Lord opens your own eyes,
To your need,
And you are met with reality,
Jesus your King,
Knows all, sees all, and has perfect understanding,
And His decision,
Is what you truly need.

311. He Chooses

May 26, 2017

Oh to work in my sweetspot,
A prayer.
I know the Lord has given me gifts,
To use to reach many this year.

The struggle is real,
When you hit that wall.
The wall didn't break,
But you felt the hit through your core and stalled.

The fact is,
The Lord above,

Holds time in His hands,
And you are the one He loves.

He chooses.

312. Endurance

May 26, 2017

It's 8 o'clock,
And I am ready for bed,
Is this what happens,
When you have kids?

A different endurance,
In life.
Kid endurance,
Writer endurance,
School endurance,
Work endurance,
Running endurance,
Muscle endurance.

You name it,
It's endurance.
A different endurance,
In life.

313. *In The Garden*

June 3, 2017

Abba!
I love You!
The One You love,
Needs You.

The One You love,
Is waiting,
The One You love,
Is relentlessly praying,
The One You love,
Is suffering.
The One You love,
Is worshipping.
The One You love,
Is struggling.
The One You love,
Is learning.
The One You love,
Is listening.
The One You love,
Is fearlessly sharing.
The One You love,
Is strengthening.
The One You love,
Is clearly seeing.
The One You love,
Is hearing.
The One You love,
Is agonizing.
The One You love,
Is serving.

The One You love,
Is submitting.

Abba!
The One You love,
Needs You.
Shining Your face from above.
I love You.
So thankful,
I am the one You love.

314. A Promise

June 3, 2017

A promise,
You whisper in the dark,
A promise,
To assure my heart.

You are here, (**Matthew 28:20**)
You are.
I'm not to fear.
You will never be far.

You redeem, (**Romans 8:28**)
That which was lost.
You restore,
No matter the cost.

You think thoughts of peace, (**Jeremiah 29:11**)
About me.

You've given me hope for the future,
That will flow through eternity.

315. *The Lonely*

June 6, 2017

I will praise You in advance,
For everything You're about to do.
God! Your love—
Broke through.

Shining from on High,
Your face smiling down.
Looking at Your people tonight,
Loving the joyful sound.

You set the lonely in families, (**Psalm 68:6**)
Bringing so many around.
You, Lord, know the aching heart,
That needs laughter to be found.

You deliver every time,
Knowing exactly what we need.
You brought the gift of humor,
That brought everyone to their knees.

So thankful for Your loving touch,
Knowing exactly what we need.
God You set the lonely in our family,
Because they met our need.

316. *That Day*

June 6, 2017

That day will come,
It will.
Hold your heart steady,
Be still.

He will come.
He will.
Make your heart ready,
Be still.

317. *My Beloved*

June 6, 2017

The fruit of my Beloved, (**Song of Solomon 2:3**)
Is so sweet to my taste.
My desire for him is strong,
He is absolutely worth the wait.

The longing on my heart,
To be near to him.
Is a godly desire,
Deep within.

The beauty in honor,
As I seek to honor him,
Will be the overflowing reward of joy,
My heart held just for him.

318. *Too Long*

June 6, 2017

If you wait too long,
You're going to miss out on life.
If you wait too long,
One day you will wonder why,
You did.
Wait too long.

319. *Restore*

June 16, 2017

There is a time for everything, (**Ecclesiastes 3:1**)
A season for everything under the sun.
A time when You, Lord,
Restore the ones You love.

Thank You for redemption day,
You alone know the scars,
That paved the way to today.
But Jesus, You never left—You stayed.
Thank You for Your presence every day. (**Matthew 28:20**)

Oh Lord Jesus, thank You for redemption day.
I rejoice now,
Knowing how my life will change,
Loving the way You redeem my name.
Healing every wound that caused such pain.

Thank You for redemption day,
You listened intently every day,
As I whispered my prayers,
Praying for change.
Watching You move mountains that very day.

Oh Lord Jesus, thank You for redemption day.
For dying on the cross that dark day.
Freeing me to read Your word of grace,
Recognizing the truth of redemption day:
The value of a life and the amount You paid.

There is a time to redeem,
The broken season,
A time to share and listen,
With even more compassion.

A time to walk away,
For your own protection.
A time to sit and pray,
Seeking the Lord's heart through meditation.

There is a time for everything,
A season for everything under the sun.
A time when You, Lord,
Restore the ones You love.

Thank You!
Thank You!
Thank You!

320. O Lord, My God

July 2, 2017

O Lord, my God,
I love You.

I heard You calling,
In the night.
A whisper so soft,
I almost didn't hear it right.

Then I knew,
You wanted me up this night,
Seeking You,
Realizing everything will be alright.

You called out three times,
Calling me to arise.
I hesitated at first,
Wondering why.

What's the word,
You want to speak to me tonight?
O Lord, My God,
You've heard my heart's cry.
You've answered my prayer,
This night.

O Lord, my God,
I love You.
Thank You!
For revealing truth.

321. *Praying Tonight*

July 2, 2017

A name on my heart tonight.
One You are calling me to pray for.
A heart to be ignited shining bright,
Reaching those in their midst with light.

Boldly moving in their gift,
Not holding back,
Realizing its this,
Not focusing on what they lack,
But recognizing they fit,
Right where they are at,
With the truth of Jesus Christ on their lips.

It's when they share what they know,
Their heart begins to grow,
Because it gets ignited with light,
Impacting all those in sight.

If only they knew,
Their impact on some,
They probably would keep going,
Reaching out to that last one.

Never knowing how that one word,
Would bring,
Comfort and assurance,
To those suffering.

Praying tonight,
They'd recognize,
How much You love them,
And they have nothing to hide.
Free to roam,
Reflecting the light,
Shining, filled.
With Jesus Christ.

Fill them with Your Holy Spirit,
So they boldly reach their world.
Thank You for shining Your face on them,
Answering those prayers, unheard.

322. Listening

July 6, 2017

I want to hear Your voice so clear,
Moments when I think I hear.
But then when I want to move forward,
Lord! That stupid door.

I try and hear when the message is given,
When worship is sung,
And hearts are rejoicing,
When words are shared,
My ears are listening,
For when You Lord are clear
Speaking to me regarding,
What You placed on my heart these past couple of years.

Seriously.

Words I already wrote down,
Seem to pop up here and there.
I am learning how to listen.
I don't have it all down, maybe sometime this year.

But then I had a moment,
When I was like,
"I think this word is for myself.
I needed to be reminded of this word tonight."

You spoke through them all.
It all pretty much fit.
The words ingrained on my heart,
Where they fit.

When people are listening intently,
Expecting You Lord to speak,
They will walk away knowing,
You, Lord, gave them exactly what they need.

323. Simple Trust

Psalm 131
July 29, 2017

Simple trust in the LORD,
Is what you need right now,
In order to live in one accord.

Not haughty hearts,
Or lofty eyes.
Concerning yourself with matters,
To great as you lie.

But calm and quiet your soul,
Like a weaned child with his mother.
Like a weaned child should be your soul,
Trusting the LORD.

Hope in the LORD,
Our eternal Rock.
The surest foundation for your foot,
As you walk.

324. *The Knowledge of Perfect Love*

August 2, 2017

You know my every step, (**Psalm 139:1**)
My every breath.
When I stand up or sit down, (**Psalm 139:2**)
You know my every thought before it's said.

Your knowledge of my life,
Comes from a perfect eye.
I can't quite grasp this love,
That pours onto my sinner soul tonight.

What gets me,
Is You see Your Son,
Every time You look at me.

I'm covered with His love.
His death on the cross.
His shed blood.
And that's all You see,
My sinner soul forgiven,
Full of righteousness and purity.

Why me?

Every day of my life, (**Psalm 139:16**)
You fashioned in Your book.
Your perfect pure eyes,
Saw what others overlooked.

How precious are Your thoughts, (**Psalm 139:17**)
About me,
More numerous than the sand, (**Psalm 139:18**)
Covering the floor of the sea.
Thank You, Lord,
For smiling upon me.

O Lord, You know me, (**Psalm 139:23**)
But continue to search,
I want to walk in the fear of the Lord,
I have to obey Your Word.

I am right before You,
Solely because of Your Son.
O thank You for knowing my need,
When I thought I had none.
And in that, Lord, I can never flee,
From the knowledge of perfect Love.

ABOUT THE AUTHOR

Alysa VanderWeerd is also the editor of the devotional, *Mountaintop Mornings*. She has written bible study curriculums for the Jr. High ministry at Harvest Christian Fellowship—Pastor Greg Laurie, on: Psalm 16:11, the book of James, and the book of Revelation.

She has her Bachelors in History with a minor in English from the University of California- Irvine. She has her Master of Arts in History from the University of California- Riverside; and is currently working on her Doctorate in Education in Community Care and Counseling: Family and Marriage from Liberty University.

Alysa lives in Southern California. She loves camping at the beach with her family, running, and working on wood projects.
For more about Alysa, visit relentlessprayer.org.

Printed in the United States
By Bookmasters